D1180686

LIVERPOOL
UNIVERSITY

LIBRARY

PO BOX 95
LIVERPOOL L19 0LB

INFANT CLASSROOM BEHAVIOUR

NEEDS, PERSPECTIVES AND STRATEGIES

By
Sue Roffey and Terry O'Reirdan

David Fulton Publishers
London

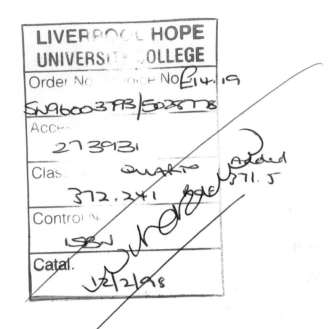

LIVERPOOL HOPE
UNIVERSITY COLLEGE
Order No
ance No £14.19
SN96003PB/5025778
Acc
2739131
Clas.
372.241
371.5
Control
ISBN
Catal.
12/2/98

David Fulton Publishers Ltd
2 Barbon Close, London WC1N 3JX

First published in Great Britain by
David Fulton Publishers 1997

Note: The right of the authors to be identified as the authors of this work has been asserted by them in accordance with the Copyright, Designs and Patents Act 1988.

Copyright © Sue Roffey and Terry O'Reirdan

British Library Cataloguing in Publication Data

A catalogue record for this book is available from the British Library

ISBN 1–85346–446–5

All rights reserved. No part of this publication may be reproduced, stored in a retrieval system or transmitted, in any form, or by any means, electronic, mechanical, photocopying, recording or otherwise, without the prior permission of the publishers.

Typeset by The Harrington Consultancy Ltd.
Printed in Great Britain by Bell & Bain Ltd., Glasgow

CONTENTS

Special notes Throughout the book we have alternated the use of 'he' and 'she' for individual children but in line with the majority of infant teachers have consistently referred to the teacher in the feminine form.

Where the term 'parents' is used it is intended to incorporate all those who care for the child.

A hand pointer (☛) is used in the text to indicate practical strategies and ideas.

FOREWORD

The first days at school are unique: they are a watershed, the first steps on a journey towards independence, self-knowledge and discovery of the wider world of learning. It is crucial for the success of that journey that the adults who share the responsibility for nurturing, guiding and educating our children should be able to work together.

During these early years children have a steep learning curve. The skills and knowledge they develop depend on maturation and the experiences and opportunities available to them. They learn to respond to the environment around them and this influences their behaviour.

Establishing clear routines and expectations, using every opportunity to make learning an exciting, stimulating and rewarding experience can ensure that the early years are a time of developing self-confidence, enquiring minds and the skills to enable the potential in each child to be fulfilled.

This book looks at a range of strategies to enable teachers, parents, carers and children to make the most of those early formative years. Strategies are suggested for dealing with problems that may arise, and examples of good practice are shared.

The authors do not claim to have all the answers, but they have excellent ideas and practical advice to offer teachers in establishing good behaviour in the infant classroom and meeting the needs of those children who find it more difficult to settle into the learning environment.

I would like to commend this book to you.

Jacky Tonge

Jacky Tonge
Director of Education Services
London Borough of Haringey

ACKNOWLEDGEMENTS

Firstly, we would like to thank all of the teachers and pupils in the London Borough of Haringey with whom we have worked over the years, and who have provided us with the impetus and enthusiasm to write this book. Some of these pupils have helped with the illustrations.

In particular we would like to thank the following schools who have given so generously of their time and expertise and where photographs have been taken: St Mary's C of E Infants School; South Harringay Infants School; Stamford Hill Primary School.

Secondly, we would also like to thank colleagues from the Education Support Service, Haringey Education Psychology Service and others who read draft copies of chapters in process. The following individuals fed back advice and constructive criticism on the completed work: Rae Gutman, Sue Davies, Mollie Bird, John Thornburn, Terry McKenzie, Priscilla Webster and Angie Holmes. Sue's SENCO cluster group also provided ideas and support.

The London Borough of Haringey gave support for an original joint project on which this work was based, and has given permission to use some of the original material.

Lastly, a very big thank you to Angie Holmes for the photography, to David Roffey for his time, patience, and technical expertise and to our respective families for their patience and support whilst our attention was focused on the writing of this book.

Some of the illustrations in the book are adapted from ClickArt Copyright © 1984–1995 T/Maker Co, used with permission.

Children live what they learn

If children live with criticism,
They learn to condemn

If children live with hostility,
They learn to fight

If children live with ridicule,
They learn to be shy

If children live with shame,
They learn to feel guilty

If children live with encouragement,
They learn confidence

If children live with praise,
They learn to appreciate

If children live with fairness,
They learn justice

If children live with security,
They learn to have faith

If children live with approval,
They learn to like themselves

If children live with acceptance and friendship,
They learn to find love in the world.

CHAPTER 1

INTRODUCTION

This book takes an overall perspective on infant behaviour. Rather than offering a single approach or a specific strategy to deal with children's difficult behaviour it clarifies all those factors which must be taken into account when promoting positive behaviour in the infant school. The message is that it is the 'whole package' that makes the difference.

Here we clarify the rationale and underlying philosophy of the book. A major theme is that although not all behaviour is learnt there is a learning component to all behaviour with which teachers can work. We share some of the excellent practice that has been developed in schools to help children learn to behave well. This is set within a framework which addresses the needs not only of children, but also of their parents and teachers. The contents of the book have a sequence, outlined in this section, which first deals with the promotion of positive behaviour for all young children and then looks at individual needs. The goal of promoting positive behaviour is ultimately the development of self management. The foundation stones for this must be addressed, if not from infancy, then from children's earliest days in school.

The skills of teachers

Most young children settle well into school life. They are generally happy, make friends easily, are responsive to teachers and enjoy learning. Such a positive situation does not come about by chance – it is due to the experiences and learning that have taken place in the pre-school years and crucially to the welcoming environment of the school and the many skills of teachers. It is a mammoth and often unrecognised task that confronts the reception class teacher who has to gather together thirty or so disparate, small, mainly egocentric beings and help them become a coherent group, aware of each other, able to cooperate and collaborate, listen, pay attention and learn. It is to those teachers' unsung credit that by the time children have been in school a year, most of them have developed the required skills to work and play together and have learned behaviour which is appropriate for school.

This is not true, unfortunately, for everyone. Some children find it more difficult to settle into school life because they have not learned skills which promote cooperation and positive social interactions. Clear guidance and teaching is required to help them replace the repertoire they bring with them with more rewarding behaviours and help them make the most of being in school. Their very first experiences in the classroom and playground will make a difference to how they view themselves within the school context and to their expectations of others.

Teachers cannot be expected to change children's behaviour overnight or make up for all the deprivations they might be experiencing. Teachers do not, however, always fully realise that their classroom might be the only place where a child is encouraged to think about him or herself positively, where there is security, safety, consistency and a sense of purpose. Although there may not be immediate changes in behaviour, a daily smile of welcome may make more difference than the teacher will ever know. There are times when teachers need reminding of the good work that they are already doing.

Schools make the difference

The research on effective schools mirrors our own experiences in working with a wide variety of institutions. The ethos, organisation and working policies in a school make a significant difference to how children's behaviour is perceived and what is put in place to develop appropriate classroom behaviours for both groups and individuals. In the most effective schools there is planned promotion of positive behaviours which takes account of the needs of parents and teachers as well as children. In the less effective schools there is little consistency of approach amongst staff who tend to react to individual instances of difficult behaviour. Because of the anxiety and confusion surrounding what to do about 'difficult kids', teachers may look to others to blame and refer most quickly to outside agencies for support. These are the schools who are also most likely to reject and exclude children.

Limiting difficulties by teaching behaviour

The rise in the number of children who are being excluded from school at a very young age is of both local and national concern. This book does not attempt to explore in any depth the many and complex reasons for this. The focus is on the ways in which schools and teachers have managed successfully to help children develop more appropriate interactions and limit behavioural difficulties in the classroom and the playground. Teachers are encouraged to think about behaviour in terms of what the child needs to learn and how the child will be taught, asking questions such as:

- Do children understand what behaviours are required in the classroom?
- Are they able to do what is being asked of them?
- Do they have an understanding of why they are being asked to behave in certain ways?
- Is cooperation in the child's perceived interests?

In order to behave in ways which win teacher approval, children need to know what it is that they have to do, have the skills to do it, and feel good about complying. Those children who can't cooperate because they are distressed, angry and feeling bad about themselves and their experiences of the world, need opportunities to learn to feel safe, comfortable, and successful in school and be able to think about themselves more positively. While it may be difficult to evaluate how well this learning is taking place it is nevertheless an outcome of the approaches, efforts and actions of teachers.

An affective curriculum

Throughout the book the importance of the 'affective curriculum' is emphasised: how children come to understand and express their own feelings and begin to learn to understand and empathise with those of others. Social and emotional development can be accelerated within the classroom in the same way as cognitive development, by teaching and mediating experiences for children, helping them to understand and giving them skills to move forward. Teachers often try to change behaviour by resisting children's expression of their emotions. Acknowledgement is often a better response in that it makes the child feel that he or she has been 'heard'. This also takes up less personal emotional energy for the adult. The feelings that teachers often have when dealing with difficult behaviour are also acknowledged and ways in which teachers might feel supported are discussed.

The Code of Practice for Special Educational Needs

This book is concerned primarily with promoting positive behaviour in young children, often at a whole school and whole class level. Stage One of the Code is identification of need for an individual child. This is where the classteacher makes minor adaptations in her approach and gathers more information. The individual approaches and strategies suggested in this book are meant to be implemented either at Stage One or in a more formal way with an individual education plan (EP) at Stage Two. It is not our intention to address the needs of those more damaged children whose emotional and behavioural difficulties are long-term and entrenched. In our experience, however, where a consistent and positive response to difficulties is in place at Stage Two, there is often a marked improvement in behaviour, making further stages unnecessary.

The outline and sequence of chapters

Differences between children when they begin school

Chapter 2 examines a wide range of pre-school experiences and how these affect the way children relate to other people, think about themselves and their abilities, share the values and aspirations of the school and know how to access the activities on offer. Chapter 3 looks at the levels of development which might be seen in an infant classroom especially with regard to emotional and social maturity and the impact this has for learning appropriate behaviour. A checklist of skills which might normally be expected from a five year old is provided so that teachers can quickly ascertain concerns and possible targets for intervention.

Teacher perspectives and teacher needs

Chapter 4 explores different ways in which behaviour might be thought about and how this affects teacher confidence in dealing with difficulties. There is an emphasis on factors to take into account when considering how children learn and which approaches may be useful in teaching behaviour. Chapter 5 looks at what teachers need in order to be most effective in the classroom and limit personal stress. Ways in which these needs might be met, including a 'framework of support' are discussed.

The needs of parents and children

It is very evident that those schools which put a great deal of thought and effort into their communication with parents also have a better record of managing behaviour. Chapter 6 is therefore devoted to the needs of parents and is illustrated by outlining some ways in which schools have promoted greater understanding and collaboration, especially across class, cultural and other differences. Schools are encouraged to think through their initial discussions with parents about behavioural concerns. An outline for a Stage One interview is included. Maslow's Hierarchy of Needs is used in Chapter 7 as a framework to identify and prioritise children's needs when they start school. Ways in which these might be met are considered.

Settling into school: taking action to promote positive behaviour

Many schools think very carefully about how children may be helped to settle into school. Chapters 8 and 9 look at the strategies that some teachers have developed to clarify expected behaviour, teach routines and give positive feedback for success. We consider the practicalities of how children can be encouraged to cooperate with adults and with each other. There is a strong focus on self-concept and self-esteem, helping the child to make sense of what is being asked and making things relevant and meaningful. All children need to fit in with the group and feel that they belong, but also to feel special and accepted as individuals. When there is a clear sense of order and fairness within the class which is communicated well to everyone, it is easier for children to maintain a commitment to the structure and routines.

When difficulties arise

Chapter 10 deals with conflict and the importance of teaching children skills of conflict management so that they can sort out minor differences themselves. There is also guidance as to when adult intervention might be appropriate and when not, including what to do about bullying behaviour. 'Circle Time' activities are particularly relevant here in raising children's self-esteem and in helping them think through ways of dealing with difficulties that arise in everyday interactions. Ways in which to de-escalate a possible confrontation are also discussed.

Finally, in Chapter 11 we come to the section on children who are particularly hard to manage. This chapter looks at assessment and intervention at Stage Two of the Code of Practice for Special Educational Needs. Whereas the rest of the book is primarily about strategies for the whole class and for groups of children, here the major focus is on the learning needs of the individual child who is having difficulty. We offer a framework to clarify a child's learning needs with respect to behavioural intervention and make suggestions both for overall approaches and direct strategies. Ideas can be selected or developed to form the basis of Stage Two individual education plans. Incorporated into this chapter are ideas for immediate management strategies for specific situations. These may not necessarily be part of a longer term learning programme but enable the teacher to have ways of dealing with crises in the classroom.

Although it is tempting for teachers to turn immediately to this section with a particular child in mind, it is stressed that the ideas and strategies found here will be more effective if they are consistent with a whole school approach to positive behaviour management. Teachers who work in less positive environments may, however, find much that is helpful here in forming their own responses to children who are hard to manage.

Using the ideas and activities

The major impetus for writing this book is to share the many excellent strategies that have been developed in schools to deal with infant classroom behaviour. This not only promotes the development of good practice for all children but also ensures that those children who do genuinely need a high level of long-term support are clearly identified as those who have the most entrenched difficulties. Pro-active measures, early strategies and structured IEPs at Stage Two, implemented consistently over time, will indicate when more specific and/or intensive intervention really is necessary

Many of the activities suggested will be common practice for many teachers. Although there may be some innovatory ideas, much of what is suggested is not new. What we hope to highlight is how these activities can meet several different learning needs and ultimately how they promote positive behaviour within the classroom.

Different teachers have different styles, and individuals will need to work within the framework of a whole school policy, in ways in which they feel most comfortable. Teachers could perhaps choose those activities which address the needs of their present class and fit in with their own way of teaching. Having said that, it's worth trying something new once in a while, or revisiting old strategies in a different way or at a different time. Some things may work very well with some children but not necessarily with everyone.

Clarity, consistency and calmness

As one teacher commented 'It's not only what you do that ensures something is effective but the consistency with which you do it and the ability to stay calm enough in order to carry it through'. It is worth adding that it is the clarity that the teacher has in knowing what it is they are trying to achieve and how specific they are able to be in devising strategies and approaches to achieve it that also makes the difference.

Onto self-management

Ultimately, a child – everyone – needs to be able to choose to behave in certain ways in certain situations; in ways which are at best beneficial and at least cause minimal damage to themselves and others. Amongst the skills and attributes this requires are:

- self-awareness
- self-confidence
- self-esteem
- an understanding about feelings and ways of expressing these
- an understanding that there are links between perceptions, feelings and actions
- empathy, together with an appreciation that people have different perspectives

- an understanding that there are choices
- an internal locus of control
- decision making abilities
- effective communication skills.

Some of these skills and attributes are not often attained by the most experienced adult let alone a small child. You will see from the examples here in this book that there are efforts by many teachers to address these prerequisites for effective self-management. They are, however, not routinely part of the curriculum in schools. If we want to see greater cooperation between teachers and pupils and improved relationships throughout the education system, then the process must at least begin in the infant classroom.

CHAPTER 2

PRE-SCHOOL EXPERIENCES

Children don't bring only their lunchboxes and their gym shoes to school: they bring along a very large package of experiences, expectations, knowledge, skills and understanding. All of these things will effect how they learn, how they behave, how they relate to other people and what they think about themselves. By the time children reach their first day at school many of their ideas about themselves and the world around them will be well established. They will have developed a 'construct' of their own reality and will try to make sense of their new experiences in a way which fits in with what they understand. This chapter sets out to explore the range of factors that may affect children's behaviour when they first come to school.

'Labels'

Labels are the messages about ourselves that we have been given by other people, firstly by our parents and then others. They influence in a big way the image we have of the person we are, how we behave, what we can and cannot do and what is to be expected of us. These labels are very sticky indeed. As adults we all still carry around a selection of labels that were handed to us, some of them from a very early age. Some we may have worked hard to cast off, others we may quite happily live up to throughout our lives. They are about how we see ourselves functioning in the world.

Labels that have been given to children before they come to school might include:

- 'clever little thing'
- 'a right nuisance'
- 'very independent'
- 'never does as she's told'
- 'really very musical'.

Each child will have an idea of what this label means in terms of what other people expect. A four year old girl who is often told by her mother that she is 'so helpful' is likely to be the one to get up and tidy the classroom as soon as she is asked. The five year old boy who understands that being 'a tough kid' means getting involved in lots of rough and tumble play may be very surprised to find that he gets into trouble as soon as he gets into a school playground for being 'too rough'.

Those few children who have been given very negative messages about themselves as small children are among those who will have the hardest time settling into the reception classroom. It may take them some time and much reinforcement to fit the positive things that teachers say about them into their idea of who they are.

☞ You can find out how children think about themselves by asking them to draw themselves in different situations or with different people and then write a sentence about this.
- 'This is me with my big sister – my big sister says I am..........................'
- 'This is me in my playgroup – in my playgroup I was ....'

Figure 2.1 My brother says I'm funny

☞ In the first place it may be better to give children a more positive idea of what labels mean: e.g. a 'tough kid' means one who is able to carry the heavy equipment around; 'slow' could be redefined as 'careful'.

Family culture

Children also come to school with an understanding about what is relevant and important or not in the world. If a child has been brought up in a strictly religious family he may have clear ideas about the importance of prayer, of fasting and of special days. There may be cultural norms which are not the same or even conflict with the culture of the school, e.g. in some cultures it is considered disrespectful for a child to look an adult in the eye. Imagine how this child might feel if told off by a teacher who says: 'Look at me when I'm speaking to you!'

It isn't just broad ethnic and religious culture that influences the way children think. It is what is considered to be 'normal' in the family in which they have spent their first five years. In some families being 'tidy' will be important and children will be expected and reminded to 'hang up your coat' or 'put your bag away'. There will be places for where things are kept and it will be quite easy for a young child to generalise this understanding into the classroom. For children from homes where neatness is not valued, or where there are no demands on children to put things away it will be something extra for them to learn at school.

In some families there will be lots of visitors all the time and the children get used to different people. Other children will have known only a very few close family members and it may be quite alarming for them to exchange this for an unfamiliar teacher and many other children.

In many families 'education' will be valued very highly indeed and there will be a great interest in what children are learning. The word 'education' however, may have different meanings to different people and some parents may be confused about the amount of 'play' that seems to go on in the classroom unless the purpose of these activities is explained.

There are also differences between families with regard to expectations and roles linked to gender. This has implications for the models that are presented to children and expectations about how to behave to be a 'proper little girl or little boy'. This issue may be one that infant teachers may find particularly hard to come to terms with in the classroom.

Opportunities to learn

There is a considerable body of research which supports the value of nursery education for all and it is an issue which is rarely off political agendas. There is little doubt that the experiences children have in nursery education are of great benefit to them in their future schooling and lay down some of the fundamental concepts on which they build essential skills and knowledge. It is, however, not only formal pre-school provision which makes a difference to the amount that young children learn. This will also depend on many things including the following:

- The access that children have had to a variety of materials with which to play and experiment
- The amount of space they have had to explore
- The range of experiences that have been provided for them
- The 'mediation' of those experiences by adults in explaining things in ways which build on existing knowledge
- The encouragement they have had to experiment and try new things
- The guidance and support they have had to help them with things that have been difficult
- The opportunities that they have had to watch and learn from others
- The interactions they have had with adults and with other children.

Some children will have had much less opportunity than others and may need some help to know what to do with all the new things that they find in the infant classroom. Others may expect to get into trouble for 'touching'

9

things and will be hesitant. Others will be overwhelmed or excited and start off by flitting from one thing to another. Children who have had few pre-school opportunities to learn may quickly feel a failure in school if this isn't recognised and some steps taken to ensure that they have initial success:

☞ Children will focus better if they are offered a restricted choice of activity with variety over time.
☞ Opportunities to practise the same skill are valuable – e.g. a table with several different puzzles.
☞ Some children may need guidance to extend their play, e.g. having an adult in the home corner for a while 'joining in', may encourage longer, more complex sequences of pretend play.
☞ Some children need to be able to stand and watch before trying things out.
☞ Talking with children about what they are doing extends their vocabulary and their conceptual understanding.
☞ Some children may have problems initially with two channel information. They can't do things and listen at the same time. Verbal input from adults needs to be brief and direct.
☞ If a child doesn't appear to understand, it is often helpful to relate what is being said to what is already familiar.

Listening

Some children will have had lots of practice at listening. They will know that when an adult looks at them and speaks directly to them they are expected to pay attention. They may have learned that it is to their advantage to listen because good things might be about to happen. They might have had stories read to them from a young age and enjoyed this very much.

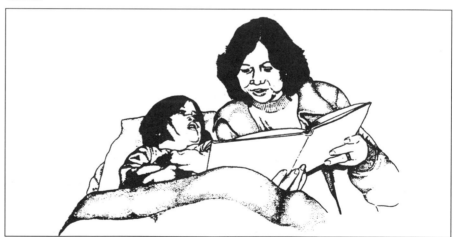

Figure 2.2 Some children will have had lots of practice listening

Some children, perhaps those who have lived in large noisy families, may not be used to listening to quiet voices and will take much more notice if someone speaks loudly. A few children may be alarmed by that very same loud voice.

There is a perception element to all our senses and we choose from the stimulation around us what we pay attention to. Some children will have had multiple auditory input from television, traffic noise and general chatter.

They may not always know what the teacher wants them to listen to unless they are given other clues.

Many children up to the age of seven – as many as one in three – experience 'conductive' hearing loss at some time, usually caused by 'glue-ear'. Where this is severe or chronic it may have prevented them from learning good listening habits. Often the difficulty is not quickly diagnosed and parents may complain that their child 'doesn't take any notice' or 'listens when she feels like it'. Children with such a hearing loss may not realise when they are being spoken to, especially when the sound comes from the back or the side of them, or they may not be able to work out what the words mean.

☞ Adults will need to make sure that they speak to such children face to face. Children will then know they are expected to listen and have extra clues to what is being communicated by watching people's mouths and expressions as they speak.

Language

Children usually pick up many of the clues which help them understand what is expected in the classroom from what is being said. It is an enormous advantage for children to have had opportunities, both at home and in nursery provision, to experience what could be termed a 'language rich environment'. It enhances the extent of their vocabulary, their skills in understanding, their ability to ask questions, their confidence in expressing their needs and feelings, their skills in using words to work things out for themselves, and their pleasure in playing and working with other children.

Some children are exposed to very little 'interactive' language. They may have spent a lot of time in front of the television where language is in one direction only; some may have parents or carers who have not realised the importance of talking with their very young children or who have been so preoccupied with other concerns that it has not been a priority. Some parents are naturally quiet themselves and not used to commenting on what is going on.

For some children the first time they hear English spoken regularly is when they arrive for their first day in school. If they have had many opportunities to become fluent in their own language then they will already know about the importance and various functions of words and with appropriate teaching and classroom experiences are likely to learn English as their second language quite quickly. It is those children who have limited experience or delay in their first language who will be at a double disadvantage when they have to learn a second language at school.

☞ Spoken language supported by visual, gestural, physical or contextual clues is very valuable for children: it helps those with restricted language skills and extends the language of the more able.

☞ Giving children lots of opportunities and encouragement to develop language skills is something that infant teachers usually manage to great effect. For those children with more difficulty a focused approach to language which gives opportunities to learn and practice new language may be more productive than introducing many new concepts in a short time.

☞ Teachers who are very concerned about a child's level of language should first of all ask parents about whether they have similar concerns and about the results of any hearing tests.

☞ A referral to a speech and language therapist may also be useful, especially if there is a severe delay or the child's language construction is unusual.

Occasionally the language that a child has learned from the people around them is unacceptable in school. If a child suddenly uses 'bad language' they will need to be told simply, quietly and probably several times, that those words are not for use in school. Being very judgmental with small children about swearing isn't very helpful and a big shocked response could be quite rewarding in the amount of attention it provides: it may reinforce the behaviour, if not with the teacher, then with other children.

Involvement and participation

Those children who have had the benefit of stimulating pre-school provision will have had opportunities to participate in activities with adults and with other children. Some parents also make a habit of involving their children in a wide variety of activities. Some of these will just be joining in with what a parent is doing or being given things to do with other children.

There are other children for whom 'being good' may have become synonymous with 'getting on with something quietly on their own'. Wanting attention has been seen as an unwelcome 'demanding' behaviour.

There are many social skills inherent in cooperative activities, listening, watching, paying attention, turn-taking, waiting and sharing. Children who have had practice at these behaviours and have seen that they are in their best interests will be motivated to collaborate because in their experience good things come out of it.

☞ Those children who have not had opportunities to participate will need to be taught collaborative skills in the same way as being taught other things.

Expectations children may have of adults

Happily, most children see adults as people who help and look after them. Some children have spent all their pre-school years with just one or two adults and may be very unsure how to relate to new people once they come to school: they may be very shy and lacking in confidence at first. Some children may have been indulged and expect adults to be there to do everything for them: it may be difficult for reception class teachers to warm to such little tyrants but these children need to learn more appropriate ways of interacting just the same as the less confident children – these children will learn this from their peers just as much as they learn it from the teachers.

Whereas some parents and carers have shown pleasure and delight in all the achievements that their children have made, others have been far more critical and hard to please. Teachers walk a fine line between acknowledging effort and success but also building skills to a higher level of attainment. Children who have been told too often that what they do is useless or not good enough may have given up trying too hard. Children who think that they don't have to do much to gain accolades will not know that they are not trying hard enough.

There are those children for whom adults, of both or either gender, may represent reasons for fear or helplessness or lack of trust. It will take time and patience to convince such children that there are some adults with whom they can feel safe, who always try to do what they say they will do, who give messages that children are likeable and valued. Children may test out such adults for many reasons: they do not fit in with their own constructs, they are a safer place for directing anger and distress or they are only used to a much harsher discipline to 'behave'. They may want to know: 'Will you still like me if I'm bad?' Teachers can respond by constantly referring to the *behaviour* that is unacceptable, not by rejecting the child.

Children who are used to being hit for not cooperating with adults will have learned that this is a way to exert power. They may also have been encouraged by adults to 'stand up' for themselves in this way. When teachers in school tell them off for hitting it does not fit it with what their life experiences have taught them, and they may become confused and uncertain. It will take time, reminders and encouragement for their behaviour in school to change.

Expectations about other children

Most children starting school will have had at least some opportunities in playgroup or nursery school to play with other children. They will have learned about what this entails, what is enjoyable about it, how to explore play situations with others and what might cause conflict. It is very likely that they will also have had to deal with some conflict and will have experimented with ways of sorting things out either by themselves, with others or with the help of adults.

The extent of other children's experiences may be limited to their siblings. Their knowledge of interactions will therefore be influenced by whether there are several siblings, how old they are and where they fit into the family with regard to position. The eldest child may seem more responsible towards other children, perhaps be more serious or want to take the lead in games. Youngest children may be quite dependent or passive or wilful because they have been indulged a little.

There will be a few children starting school who have had almost no opportunity to mix with their peers and will have to learn from scratch some basic social skills which enable them to join in with games. Children who have had positive experiences with adults who have modelled and taught them a range of useful social skills will transfer these skills to school situations without difficulty.

Routines

There is a routine to most infant classrooms, things happen in some sort of order and most children quickly understand that this is the case. Other children will not be used to this and will have led a much more flexible life style with far fewer routines. Such children may be much more able to cope with change and the unexpected but they may also find it takes them more time to wait for something or to learn that the same thing happens every day. They may not appreciate that everything they do will have an end point and will wander about from one activity to the other because they are not used to doing one thing at a time to completion. These children also find it difficult to make predictions about things happening.

☛ Children who have difficulty with routines will need reminders more often about how and when things happen in school. Pictorial day charts could be useful, or photographs for certain routines.

☛ Children could be asked if they remember 'what happens now?'

☛ They will also need to have activities which have a clear objective and to be encouraged to complete what they are doing with great praise for their achievement – whatever it is.

Getting attention

Some children have not experienced a very close, interactive relationship with the adults in their lives who have been too busy or too tired to give them much attention. Such children may be very attention seeking when they come to school. It is usually also the case that demanding children have developed negative ways of attracting attention because this is what they have discovered works best. When they are 'good' and quiet no-one takes any notice of them, but when they fuss, scream, irritate and annoy they get intense, direct, undivided attention - at least of one sort or another!

Attention is very rewarding indeed to most children and teachers have to shift the focus of attention seeking behaviour by giving attention by way of smiles, praise and other rewards for the behaviour they want to see for each child in the classroom.

For some children this will need a highly consistent and 'over the top' intervention because they have been used to several years of reinforcement for negative attention seeking.

Messages about school, teachers and learning

When children walk into school on their first day they will have a number of expectations about what school is going to be like, what teachers do, and what happens in the classroom. This will be based on the visits they may have made, the things that their parents will have said and perhaps information from older brothers and sisters. These messages will hopefully serve to make them feel excited, curious, and comfortably secure about starting school. Sadly this is not going to be the positive story for all children, some of whom may be scared, fearful of failing, and worried about getting into trouble or not knowing what to do.

With the best of intentions some parents will have given their children messages which do not accurately reflect the reality in today's classroom. They may tell children that they will have to do as they are told once they go to school with an unspoken 'or else'. They may have said that it is a place for work and not for play and be critical of both children and their teachers when they bring home creative work or do not bring home pages of sums.

☛ The messages that parents are given about what happens in school before the children actually start is therefore crucial.

(For more detail on this see Chapter 6, 'The Needs of Parents').

Summary

Many young children come to school for the first time having had experiences and opportunities during their early years which help them to settle quickly and easily into an educational environment. Others may need support to do this.

14

PUTTING THE RISING FIVE IN CONTEXT

What do children bring with them to school?

- experiences of interactions - with adults & peers
- an understanding of what will happen if ....
- knowledge of how best to get high quality attention
- ideas of what is and isn't important
- experiences of play
- views of themselves within the context of the family
- a certain self-image
- varying skills of communication
- feelings of fear or security
- different levels of development and skill acquisition
- a developmental level which is still basically egocentric
- messages about school and learning - making them excited, eager and curious or fearful and anticipating failure.

Many young children come into school with experiences which help them to settle - others may need the following:

- encouragement to think of themselves more positively
- help in understanding what is expected of them
- to be taught skills to help them thrive in the infant classroom
- to learn to get attention by positive behaviours
- to learn to trust school staff as people who are kind and 'safe'
- experiences that make them feel that learning is exciting
- to feel that they can be successful learners

CHAPTER 3

DEVELOPMENT AND BEHAVIOUR

Development is, by and large, sequential - things happen in a certain order. Children usually go through the babbling phase before they begin to use words, for instance. These stages are more or less the same for all children but there are differences in the rate and ease with which developments occur. All aspects of development are affected by the interaction of many factors – biological and genetic, environmental, social and cultural and the child's own personality. Some of these factors and interactions inhibit and others enhance aspects of development. It is a highly complex process and researchers are continuing to unravel its many mysteries. The following is an account of some aspects of development, particularly social and emotional development, which may be useful to teachers in understanding children's needs and behaviour in the classroom.

Differences in development

Within an infant classroom there will be children who are almost one year older than others; there will also be children who are generally well advanced for their age and others who are slower. It is likely there will be children who have age appropriate development in some areas of their functioning but not all. These differences in development at such a young age, especially in the reception classroom, can be significant in what can reasonably be expected from each individual. Despite teachers' knowledge of these facts, the demands of the curriculum, league tables and parents' wishes may very well make them feel pressured to teach children to run before they have learned to walk!

This section sets out to look at certain pathways of development up to school age and what influences there might be which affect these. This will, hopefully, assist teachers to understand certain behaviours in terms of developmental levels and suggest appropriate expectations and teaching targets. We are focusing primarily on emotional, social and 'moral' development, including the development of a 'sense of self' but acknowledge that all aspects, in particular language and cognitive development, also have a major impact on classroom behaviour.

Emotional development

When we are talking about emotional development we are concerned with:

- the feelings children have
- how they express their emotions

- how they understand what they feel
- their control of impulses
- their awareness and understanding of others' emotions.

The feelings children have

Babies express some basic emotions very clearly and immediately. By the time they are a few weeks old they appear to experience happiness, interest, surprise, fear and anger. As babies become toddlers they normally express a great deal of pleasure in life although increasingly the urge for independence can lead to other feelings, such as frustration and fury! The range of emotions children display increases in line with other aspects of their development. Anger and sadness are often confused for the pre-school child and it is our experience that this remains true for many distressed children in the infant school. It appears that hitting out in anger is a more manageable response than dealing with overwhelming misery. This is sometimes mirrored in grieving adults. Young children find it very difficult to understand that it is possible to feel two emotions at the same time and some researchers have found that they may be over seven before this concept is firmly embedded (Harter and Buddin, 1987).

This is particularly important for teachers to remember when they want to convey disapproval of behaviour together with warmth and acceptance towards the child. It may help to remind the child that they can feel two things at once themselves, e.g. pleasure and fear on a fairground ride.

Feelings of pride and shame are socially and culturally determined and initially depend on the direct approval or disapproval of important adults in the child's life. Children don't arrive in school necessarily with the same constructs as the teachers. It isn't until an average age of seven that feelings of pride and shame are internalised and not dependent on adult responses. It follows that a child's relationship with his teacher is a crucial factor in determining emotional reactions to approval or disapproval in the classroom.

Emotional expression and control

The first displays of emotion in babies are innate – babies everywhere cry when they are distressed, smile and gurgle when they are happy. Self-control of emotions develops gradually and unevenly and is strongly influenced by observation and imitation, sometimes known as 'social referencing'. Children at a very young age for instance, will look to their carer to ascertain whether they should be alarmed or not by a stranger. Even for much older children a calm but firm response by a significant adult will enable a distressed child to soothe themselves. Conversely, perceived anger or panic in an adult may generate those feelings in a child even though the precipitating cause is unknown to them.

Certain voice qualities such as pitch, tone and loudness, convey specific emotional messages to children who may pay at least as much attention to this as to the words themselves. This highlights the need for sensitivity in the ways teachers communicate. In simple terms, an angry response to an angry child will exacerbate their lack of control. Calmness doesn't however, mean blandness. There is other evidence to suggest that affective engagement with a child – a clear but controlled expression of feelings, is also a powerful factor in changing behaviour. It is important for children of all ages to know that what they do *matters* to the important people around them.

Children under the age of three years are unable to hide what they are actually feeling and infant school children will continue to have a struggle covering up strong emotions. In some ways this is what makes this age group so rewarding and delightful to teach; they are often full of excitement, enthusiasm, wonder and immediacy.

Control of negative emotions, or at least the acceptable expression of them is, however, necessary if children are to be able to make and maintain positive relationships with others. It is a fine line to walk between the encouragement not to repress feelings and, on the other hand, preventing an expression of emotions which becomes overwhelming and has negative consequences for the child. Expecting children to manage this self-regulation at a young age is a tall order and some of them will take much longer than others to succeed or may not succeed at all.

What children do have, however, are increasing skills with which to express their emotions more acceptably. By school age, only very few children show they are upset by engaging their whole bodies, throwing themselves on the floor with flailing arms and legs and incoherent yelling. Anger in school, however, may be expressed by kicking or punching and it may be useful to encourage children to see control in terms of maturity. With the development of language, increased control over facial expression, fine motor co-ordination and problem solving skills they will be able to devise and have access to other strategies. (See 'Emotional Distress' in Chapter 11, 'The Hard to Manage Child').

Young children need a lot of physical closeness to express and receive warmth and affection. As they become older and secure in relationships this closeness can be expressed without such a high level of physical contact. The insecure or immature child may continue to demand or need many cuddles in school and nearly all children benefit from a friendly and respectful touch which conveys warmth. A friendly hand briefly resting on a young child's arm or shoulder when their emotions are getting out of control may help the child to reassert control themselves. Children for whom physical contact has connotations of fear may respond differently and teachers and other adults in school will need to take account of this.

The maturation of the brain, in particular the cerebral cortex, plays an important part in inhibiting behaviour and allows children to delay responding to impulse. Children in school who are very impulsive and do not appear to be able to 'think' before acting need to 'overlearn' a safer set of reactions if their impulsive behaviour is causing distress to themselves or others. As they get older they can learn to become more aware of the physical signals of emotion and which situations provoke these. This will begin to give them a 'space' of consciousness which will empower them to choose deliberate action rather than be at the mercy of impulse.

Culture and emotional expression

Increase in heart rate, respiration and brain activity are physical manifestations of emotion common to all cultures. The regulation of emotions changes with maturation but is also strongly influenced by the processes of socialisation. The ways in which feelings are communicated are channelled into socially acceptable ways. Western societies traditionally discourage displays of extreme emotion of any kind, seeing this as immature and/or unmanly (except in prescribed circumstances such as sporting events).

Children gradually learn to conform to a way of expressing their emotions in a culturally acceptable way, e.g. by the time he is six years old a child brought up in a home where 'table manners' are highly valued may have learned to just say: 'I'm not hungry today' rather than push his plate of unwelcome food away with an expression of disgust and a loud 'yuk'. In those infant schools which have a diverse cultural mix children will have learned different ways of acceptably expressing emotion and for some there may be a conflict with the expectations in school. There are also cultural and gender differences both in the manner and in the interpretation of emotional expression. Consider the little boy who is fighting back tears and about to hit out at a perceived insult: some people would interpret this as courage, others as sadness and others as anger and aggression. Being brave may also be an interpretation seen as less applicable to girls. The gender divide in emotional expression is a potential concern as girls 'act out' their angry and distressed feelings less overtly, especially as they get older. Because this does not cause teachers so much trouble in the classroom girls' emotional needs may be overlooked. Boys are also often discouraged from tearful displays of emotion and this in itself may lead to displays of aggression as an alternative.

Understanding other people's emotions

It isn't very long before babies become intensely interested in the emotional signals of others, especially parents or other carers. Positive responses from these significant people help in the development of close trusting relationships and lead to confident exploration of the world.

Figure 3.1 From an early age children are very interested in the responses of others

By the end of their first year babies can distinguish a range of emotional expressions and will often display the same emotion that is being communicated to them. By the end of their second year toddlers will respond 'egocentrically' to others' emotional states, e.g. going to comfort someone who is crying by giving them a well loved toy or blanket. By the time they are two years old children can express simple understanding of cause and effect with regard to emotions, e.g. 'broke plate, mummy cross'. The extent and development of a child's reasoning will, to a great extent, depend on the level to which comments and discussion about feelings have been included in verbal interactions. By three a child will be regularly commenting on the feelings of others as well as their own feelings and use language to try and influence or guide behaviour: 'don't cry teddy, all better now'. They also 'experiment' with emotions and try out behaviours which may evoke an emotional response. This is both positive, such as making a brother or sister laugh, or negative, such as deliberately taking away a toy. At four most children will have an understanding that desire interacts with feelings: e.g. if someone really wants a go on the slide but is given a go on the swing they might be upset rather than pleased and by six there is an even greater understanding that how someone thinks about a situation, their beliefs, perceptions and attitudes, influence both desire and emotions. Once a child has reached this stage then they are ready for more structured cognitive-behavioural interventions.

Most young children continue to remain acutely aware of the emotions and responses of important people in their lives and it is usually only when things have gone seriously awry in some way that they cease to either be aware or care – even though they may defend themselves by saying 'I don't care'. There is good evidence to suggest that children who have been abused in some way have much greater difficulty in identifying emotions in others and are less likely to display concern or empathy.

Influences on emotional development

It is impossible to adequately summarise the vast literature on this subject so we have selected a few salient points.

Negative influences

- Clearly if a child's basic emotional needs for acceptance, affection and security are not being consistently met by at least one significant person then this will have a profound effect on their development and they are likely to be amongst the most difficult children to manage.
- Children of abusive parents often have major deficiencies in their ability to express emotions and to understand other people's feelings. They also have difficulties in controlling their own aggression.
- Depressed mothers are more likely to have insecure children who find it hard to relate to others, withdraw from interactions and are at risk of behavioural problems. Even mild rejection, real or perceived, seems to be very hard for these children to cope with.
- Anger within the family can have profound effects on young children. Conflict at home can result in high levels of frustration, tension, anger and anxiety.
- When one parent leaves, young children may experience grief which is also invariably tinged with guilt and blame. Even when it is explained to them they cannot understand that they are not in some way responsible for their parents' separation. Confusion and anger are part of the grieving

process and small children have few resources to understand and manage this. The remaining parent is also often distressed and may not be tuned in to the child's needs, possibly not even talking to them about what has happened. It isn't surprising that children find school a 'safer' place to express some of these complex emotions.

● Children who haven't had opportunities for play are likely to be emotionally delayed, as this is one way children integrate their experiences and feelings. This doesn't mean that children need toys or commercially produced materials but they do need space, time, encouragement and guidance. Children from some refugee or homeless families therefore may need extra supported play situations when they first come to school.

Positive influences

Promoting a child's self-esteem, showing acceptance and warmth will all promote emotional development. Emotionally damaged children often find it very risky to establish trusting relationships and a teacher with whom they do begin to feel attached may be surprised – and maybe disheartened – by sudden rejections. Acknowledging children's feelings and talking with them about their emotions in general helps them to identify what they are feeling, gives them the language to do this and promotes a better understanding of emotion.

Figure 3.2 Talking about feelings

Parents and carers who encourage children to express positive emotion but also help them to cope effectively with negative emotions, especially conflict, enable them to explore strategies for managing their own feelings. The developing understanding of general cause and effect in relationships also enhances children's awareness of the causes of emotion.

Adults who talk about their own feelings and model positive ways of managing these also give children access to strategies for self-management, e.g. 'I feel very sad today because my cat died, I had a good cry before I came to school. I am going to put lots of photos of her in a book tonight so I can look at it sometimes and remember her.'

21

The effects of emotional development on learning ability

Those children who are emotionally distressed and whose emotional development is impaired will have much greater difficulty than others in paying attention to and taking an interest in the world around them. Those children for whom exploration is inhibited by emotions of fear of failure or anxiety about punishment will be reluctant to engage in formal learning. Such children are unlikely to develop their conceptual understanding at an optimum pace and their school attainments will fall further behind those of their peers. Teachers in junior and secondary schools will be familiar with pupils whose difficulties have become entrenched and where learning, feelings and behaviour continually interact to produce a negative downward spiral. Eventually the child becomes a young person who has little motivation to be in school and is seriously disaffected. Although this may seem ovious it is not always evident in classrooms that learning difficulties may have their root in and be maintained by a child's emotional functioning and unmet needs. If children, in their early experiences in school, can be assured of success in small ways which raise their self esteem, they may begin to be more open to the range of learning opportunities available to them. Focusing on the possible and the positive can help interactions to spiral upwards.

The importance of pretend play

The two year old child can 'pretend' to feel things and begins to use play as a way of working through emotions. The importance and significance of this is illustrated by a research study which found that 94 per cent of conversations about feelings between siblings took place within the context of pretend play. (Dunn, 1987)

When children have developed sufficient imaginative skills they can use pretend play to act out emotional issues. Dramatic and symbolic play seems to help children to integrate all of their emotional resources, to communicate their deepest feelings and to use problem-solving scenarios to work through difficulties. The infant classroom is an ideal place to facilitate this and children benefit from encouragement in both formal and informal ways to 'act out' safely. This is most often 'home corner' play but can also include puppets, miniature people, plasticine figures, art work, drama and dressing up. Observations of children during a pretend or role play session can give some helpful indications as to what might be causing concern. It is also important to give access to emotional expression to children who are having a struggle to express themselves in verbal language.

Play is also the activity in which children practice and rehearse social skills. These will be built on the models that have been available to them. If children have had models of social behaviour which are unhelpful in the school context, then they need alternatives made available to them and encouragement to copy.

Social development

Social and emotional development are closely related. Not surprisingly the development of social relationships assists children to regulate the expression of their emotions. There is evidence to suggest that the presence of someone perceived as a friend can reduce stress responses in times of anxiety. (Kamark et al, 1990).

Figure 3.3 The importance of pretend play

Children are also often excellent modifiers of their classmate's behaviour and are clear about what they will or will not tolerate. They tend to ignore children who cannot follow basic social rules or whose emotional volatility causes some alarm. For some individuals, however, this perceived rejection exacerbates anti-social behaviour and they need more support to interact positively. Rejection by classmates has a significant correlation with future mental illness so it is vital that children do learn the skills required to establish rewarding relationships. (Cowen *et al*, 1973)

Small children are very interested in the activities of others of their age and recent studies have shown that there is more awareness and interaction earlier than previously thought. The skills of social interaction would appear to be influenced by the confidence of children who have secure adult attachments, the models of pro-social behaviour that are available, adult commentary on cooperative play skills and the opportunities that exist for peer group interaction.

Between the ages of two and four there is a great increase in children's awareness of peers and their ability to interact in a collaborative way. Toddlers make frequent overtures to each other but these are momentary rather than sustained. The solitary and parallel play commonly seen in a two year old is often interspersed with a great deal of close observation of other children. This type of interaction is followed by 'associative activity' where two children are engaged with the same activity and both contribute but there is no interdependence. Between the ages of four and seven there is the development of friendships which have a greater sense of reciprocity and collaboration. Children begin to exert greater choice in playmates although proximity and opportunity are still powerful factors: e.g. your best friend may be the person who sits next to you in class. During the infant school years a friend is largely defined as someone who 'does things for you', invites you to their party or lends you their pencil. Children therefore need to develop 'helping' skills and an understanding of the need for 'give and take' in relationships. As the ability to collaborate and cooperate develops so does the ability to establish and maintain friendships. The latter is often a motivating factor for the former.

Those young children who find it easiest to have good relationships with their peers appear to be positive and accepting of others and actively include other children in play situations. Less popular individuals push their way in so that they disrupt what is going on and are often negative, both verbally and actively, towards their peers. It is what children are like *most* of the time which matters, the occasional outburst of anti-social behaviour is usually tolerated and makes little difference to a child's popularity.

Mixed age social interaction is a very valuable way of teaching small children social skills and enhancing social maturity. It is also a valuable exercise for the older child. Children with older siblings are often more socially skilled than others and sometimes the younger children in a family have a level of social development which is more advanced than their cognitive level might suggest.

Communication skills are, of course, crucial and social development can be adversely affected for those who do not have sufficient verbal or non-verbal skills for collaborative play.

Moral development

The ability to judge whether something is right or wrong is closely linked to cognitive development. A child who is generally immature may not have reached an independent understanding of the concept of rules by the time he reaches school and will therefore need this learning to be introduced and reinforced.

A well-known theorist in the area of moral development is Kohlberg. He describes three levels of moral development, with six stages.

Most children at pre-school and infant school will be operating at the pre-conventional level which is as follows:

- Stage 1, doing what you are told by those in authority and you obey their rules or risk getting into trouble.
- Stage 2, doing what is in your interest or meets your needs. Accepting that this premise is also true for others. Rightness and fairness are interchangeable concepts.

It follows that for some children there will be 'moral confusion'. They may be told by parents for instance, that it is right to retaliate to aggression but by teachers that it is wrong. In school they will get into trouble if they do fight back, at home they will get into trouble for not standing up for themselves. The concept of 'fairness' however may be useful in thinking about strategies for intervention and managing behaviour, especially in dealing with conflict.

Children at this pre-conventional level do not initially take motivation and intent into account when judging whether something is right or wrong. The outcome will be the reference by which they decide how serious something is. If a child breaks six cups by tripping over, that will be seen as of greater consequence than one cup being broken by being dropped deliberately on the floor and children believe that the punishment should be consequently more severe. There is evidence, however, to indicate that children are open to explanation and guidance at this age and able to learn that other factors are significant. This mediation is therefore an important part of teachers' response to children's behaviour.

The development of a 'sense of self'

Self-concept

Everyone has a concept of 'self' that is our personal identity. It is based on the information that we have about ourselves, in physical and academic terms, that we have received from the people and world around us. We will have ideas about how successful, attractive, clever etc we are, and about how other people may judge us.

A young child begins to develop an understanding of self from the very first moments of existence which is based on the responses and attitudes of significant care givers in their lives. By the time children start school their self-concept will be well established. One child may perceive himself to be kind, clever and a significant member of the family. Yet another who has had their every wish fulfilled may think of themselves (briefly in the school context) as all powerful!

Where needs have been met slowly or reluctantly or where there has been much criticism, negativity and little positive attention the child may believe himself to be 'naughty', 'lazy', even unloved.

Ideal self

Similarly, we each have an 'ideal self' – the self that we would like to be. This ideal self is also the outcome of the hopes, wishes, expectations and demands of significant people in our lives. The gap between self-concept and ideal self gives rise to self-esteem which is the way people feel about themselves. Although having an ideal to strive for is healthy, where there is a huge gap between our perception of ourselves, and how we (and/or others) would like us to be, our self-esteem will be low and we may give up trying as the goal appears unattainable. Conversely, where there is little apparent difference between our self-concept and ideal self we may become complacent, with little or no drive to improve.

Making sense of the world

Children develop an understanding of themselves and the world over time and will try to fit new experiences into their personal constructs of what the world is about. The meanings that are inferred from events will depend on these constructs. This may mean that teachers' initial attempts to change the way a child sees himself may be resisted as it doesn't 'make sense'. A child may, for instance, be so used to the self-concept of 'lazy' that praise for working could be dismissed as not genuine. Constructs and self-concepts do develop and alter with new experiences but it takes time and consistency for changes to be incorporated into existing schemas.

Summary

There appears to be a welcome resurgence of the recognition that a child's emotional development cannot be separated from her ability to access the cognitive curriculum in schools. There also is increasing understanding that children learn more effectively within a positive social context. This book contains much about children's self-image and the promotion of their self-esteem. This is a primary emotion as it is concerned with how the child feels about herself. Self-esteem can, however, be situation specific and we need to pay attention to how children feel about themselves in the learning

25

situation in school. Linking learning with positive emotions such as success, pride and a sense of achievement and approval cannot but help enhance motivation, promote intellectual endeavour and maintain appropriate classroom behaviour.

THE FIVE YEAR OLD

If a child is developing at an optimum rate these are the skills, abilities and level which might be seen in an infant classroom. Where a child is clearly having difficulty in one or more areas then this indicates the need for further investigation and intervention.

Language development
A child of five will usually:

- be very interested in stories
- listen attentively and then retell the main elements of a simple story in reasonable sequence
- understand and answer simple questions
- ask lots of questions including 'why?'
- follow instructions that have three or four components
- use speech that is mostly grammatically correct
- be able to indicate whether something is in the past, present or future
- be able to say name, age and sometimes birthday and/or address
- be able to identify words that rhyme
- be able to identify words beginning with certain sounds
- have a basic concept of print
- use language to provide commentary on play
- be able to describe events
- be able to make up stories
- use language to solve problems
- use language to predict – why/because constructions
- show increasing complexity in imaginative thinking
- be able to attend to someone talking while carrying on with an activity.

Physical skills
A child of five will usually:

- be fully mobile and often very energetic
- show increasing skill and co-ordination in ball games
- be able to climb and balance with increasing skill
- tune in and move to the rhythm in music
- hold a pencil in a pincer grip and draw representationally with increasing attention to detail and features
- be able to colour within outlines
- copy letters under a model.

Mathematical understanding and skills
A child of five will usually:

- count fingers with one to one correspondence
- be able to compare, sort, match and order
- recognise and use numbers to ten
- have an awareness of number operations
- recognise patterns
- have an understanding of time as it relates to the routines of the day
- use language to describe shape, position, size and quantity
- use skills to problem solve

Social understanding and skills

A child of five will usually:

- be aware of the need for rules in games
- be able to take turns with minimum of supervision
- be sensitive to what is and what is not 'fair'
- begin to recognise the need for 'give and take' in relationships
- choose some friends independently
- be able to play cooperatively with two or three other children
- have some understanding of turn-taking in conversation
- have a range of group skills e.g. know how to share attention
- play games with increasing complexity
- know the difference between fantasy and reality and play many 'pretend' games
- be able to understand jokes and have a developing sense of humour
- be independent in selecting activities but ask for help when necessary
- lend and borrow items of equipment and toys
- feed themselves competently
- undress and dress independently but may need help with fastenings
- use a toilet unaided.

Emotional understanding and behaviour

A child of five will usually:

- be enthusiastic and motivated to learn
- have a wide range of feelings though not necessarily identified clearly
- have an increasing awareness of feelings and relate these to wants
- use an increasing range of varied, complex and flexible ways of expressing emotions
- use language for emotional control and expression
- have increasing emotional control but not be able to hide feelings completely
- use play to work out emotional issues.
- have a growing sensitivity to feelings of others
- be able to show caring to pets and younger children
- be able to comfort distressed peers
- be able to say what is right and wrong depending on family and cultural values but not have internalised a moral code as yet
- continue to test boundaries from time to time
- a child of five cannot yet link perceptions, attitudes and beliefs with emotions.

CHAPTER 4

PERSPECTIVES

Here we deal with the ways in which teachers may think about the children in their class, the reasons they often give for their behavioural difficulties and the consequent responses. We explore a range of perspectives in terms of their usefulness in managing behaviour.

This chapter is not intended to be a detailed academic exploration of the many models of behaviour that exist in the literature, but looks at some ideas about children's learning with respect to behaviour.

Expectations of behaviour

Physical factors such as height, skin colour and build are all visible attributes for each child. A class photograph of any infant class shows immediately the differences in physical appearance within any particular age-group. Similarly, the personalities of pupils within a class will vary, with some pupils noisy and boisterous, others quiet and sedentary, some hardworking and eager to please, others less so. Teachers recognise all these differences as being perfectly normal but despite being able to acknowledge the heterogeneous nature of pupil personality, attainment and ability many teachers have a belief that when they start school, pupils of a certain age should know how to behave in a certain way: 'He's five now, he should be able to sit still for ten minutes'. Having allowed some time for pupils to settle into the new environment of their classroom and learn its routines, teachers soon have some 'across the board' expectations for behaviour. Those children who do not or cannot conform may present difficulties.

This is illustrated by research carried out in London by the Thomas Coram Institute, which found that teachers considered 16 per cent of 4 to 7 year old children had 'definite' behavioural problems and a further 17 per cent had 'mild problems'. There was also a marked increase in these numbers between the reception year and middle infants. (Tizard *et al*, 1988). These are worrying statistics but they beg many questions which relate to expectations, teacher perceptions and the problems that teachers might have experienced in dealing with the difficulties that were presented. When does behaviour become a problem and who is it a problem for and why?

It is often only when faced with a pupil who is having difficulty in living up to their expectations that teachers revisit their own ideas about behaviour.

Beliefs about causality

Teachers' perceptions are based on the understanding and beliefs they have about why children behave in the way they do. These ideas are fundamental in shaping their own responses and actions within the classroom towards children who do not easily conform. In our work with teachers we have come across many views on behaviour. Sometimes these views lead to a sense of helplessness, while others offer more positive ways of thinking about difficulties and suggest ways in which teachers can make a difference.

Home background

It is understandable for teachers to look first to the child's home environment as an explanation for why children are behaving as they do in school. Parenting styles and parent/child relationships are fundamental in how children see themselves, what is expected of them and their response to demands. It would be foolish to deny or to minimise this. What is less common is a recognition that most parents want the best for their children and that they often have been doing as well as they can with the knowledge, skills and resources available to them. Parents are rarely deliberately poor managers of their children's behaviour and are often distressed and bewildered by serious difficulties and are at a loss to know what to do. Sometimes they resort to strategies that make matters worse, or a cycle of rejection becomes established.

Although poor early management or damaged relationships may very well be at the root of present difficulties in school, the view 'what can you expect with parents like that' is not a very helpful way of thinking for several reasons:

- It may lead to a self-fulfilling prophecy as there are lower expectations from the start for particular children
- It may deny any positive attributes that parents do have and is unlikely to lead to the vital development of positive home-school relationships
- It disempowers the teacher since it leads to feelings of helplessness in establishing the necessary behaviour.

Parents may also be judged for not having provided what is perceived as desirable in terms of pre-school experiences. As there is bias towards particular forms of early learning experiences which mirror and support those at school, cultural and class differences can be very significant and we need to be aware of making quick value judgements. Although certain experiences undoubtedly make it easier for the child to settle into a formal educational environment, other experiences are perfectly valid.

Parents have the most significant part to play in how their child develops, but self-concept and behaviour continue to be shaped throughout life and teachers, amongst others, can be highly influential. Although children learn a very great deal in their formative years, no-one would suggest that a child stops learning at five. Neither do they stop adapting and changing ways of behaving. Building a good relationship and working with parents increases the chances that this will be a change for the better.

The child's personality

Some teachers believe that personal characteristics of the child are 'givens' and that these underlie behaviour. Teachers often speak positively about children's personal attributes such as 'kind', 'hard-working' and so on. They may also refer to other children as 'uncooperative', 'attention-seeking', 'hyperactive', 'aggressive' etc. Thinking of a pupil in these terms can be particularly unproductive if it leads to the teacher feeling that:

- they cannot change the child's basic personality
- there is therefore nothing that they can do when faced with a child's undesired behaviour
- if any changes do occur, they will be short-lived as the child will revert back to form.

The classroom as battleground

Teachers have thirty or so children whose learning needs have to be met and may feel that the disruptive behaviour of the minority prevents them from carrying out their professional responsibilities towards the others. Children who don't conform may be blamed for making the teacher's job much more difficult. Pupils may be considered as choosing not to follow the teacher's rules or directives when consideration needs to be given to whether or not they are able to, whether or not such rules make sense to them, or whether or not compliance may be a threat to their self-esteem. The predominant issue may be one of power and control and who is going to 'win out' at the end of the day. This perspective on behaviour is more commonly found in secondary schools but not unknown in infant classes.

Teachers who stick rigidly to this view may also take the breaking of their rules as a personal threat, and feel very undermined or intimidated by the behaviour of some pupils, even over minor matters. Although it is appropriate for the teacher to be 'in charge' of the class in terms of orchestrating what goes on, this more extreme view of control is unproductive in that it:

- reinforces negative stereotypes and expectations for certain individuals;
- deprives these children of essential opportunities and experiences to learn and practice the required behaviour in a staged and structured way;
- denies these children the opportunity to experience trust;
- gives little acknowledgement or feedback for positive achievements;
- influences the way other children see the child;
- doesn't address the need to develop self-concept and self-esteem;
- takes up a great deal of emotional energy;
- expects all the changes to come from the child;
- models unhelpful ways of dealing with conflict;
- can be especially damaging to children who have experiences at home which leave them feeling powerless.

The following perspectives on behaviour are usually more helpful as they seek out possible ways of implementing change.

An interactive view of behaviour

Most teachers see behaviour as the result of interactions between:

- the many things the child brings to a situation
- the demands of that situation
- the way the child is supported in making sense of expectations.

They will be looking to see what it is possible to change, either in expectations, or in context, or in the way the child thinks and feels.

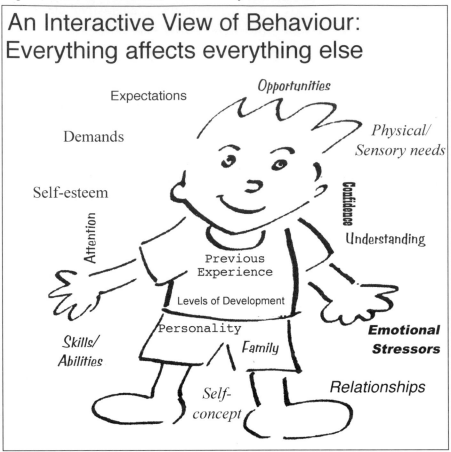

An Interactive View of Behaviour: Everything affects everything else

Figure 4.1 What can you change? How can you change it?

What can be changed

There are many possibilities within an interactive model and few factors which are not open to intervention. Teachers' decisions and actions can make an immediate difference to expectations, demands and opportunities. Teacher approaches can begin to enhance understanding, self-concept, and self-esteem.

Behaviour can be taught

Once a teacher accepts that there are factors within the situation that they can change or influence, then many different and useful approaches in teaching behaviour can come into play. The focus is on what the child needs to learn and what might be changed to enhance that learning.

Each individual has different strengths and weaknesses and this is as true of behaviour as it is of academic learning. This viewpoint is held by many teachers, and is the basis of good teaching practice. These teachers will understand that some pupils need to be taught behaviour in a more structured and planned way than others and that some children will need to have their learning more focused on particular skills than others.

THE EFFECT OF INTERRELATING FACTORS ON OUTCOMES

The story	How it is possible to inhibit escalation
Kerry is feeling overtired, she stayed up too late last night	*Initial messages to parents about the importance of sleep and how this affects children's learning*
⇩	
She had a battle with her mother over getting dressed this morning. She feels both angry and weepy as she comes to school	*The teacher notices Kerry's distress and offers a familiar, calming activity*
⇩	
The teacher gives her something to do that she hasn't seen before. New things often make her feel stupid – it's her big brother who's the clever one	*Teacher has already made a point of making positive comments about Kerry's ability and frequent opportunities to be successful*
⇩	
Kerry thinks this will be too difficult. She starts to try and play with the person sitting next to her instead. This person rejects her overtures	*Collaborative working and peer support is routinely encouraged*
⇩	
So Kerry scribbles on her book	*Teacher gives clear, calm message about unacceptable behaviour, but acknowledges Kerry's distress. Offers opportunity to make amends and informs of future consequences if it happens again*
⇩	
It's nearly half-term	*Staff aware of everyone's exhaustion and the need to support each other*
⇩	
This morning the teacher has had: i) a disappointment over her plans for the holiday and ii) an 'unsupportive' conversation with a colleague. Kerry's aggression is the last straw	*Teacher is aware of her own needs and is taking care of her stress levels as much as she can*
⇩	
She shouts (like Kerry's mum did this morning)	*Speaking quietly to children is part of the school ethos and expected teacher behaviour*
⇩	
She also touches on Kerry's sensitivities about not being 'clever'	*Teacher is aware of negative labelling*
⇩	
Kerry doesn't think – she reacts. She throws the first thing that comes to hand. It happens to be something breakable from a 'showing' table. Someone gets hurt	*Classroom layout takes account of safety issues*
⇩	
Kerry has a fixed term exclusion	*School policies have clear criteria for exclusion. Re-integration is planned positively with all involved*

Children learn behaviour in the same way as they learn cognitive skills

Simply being alive is a learning experience. Sometimes this learning is intentional, in which case there is a teaching element. Sometimes the learning is unintentional and the outcome not always so welcome. The following is by no means an exhaustive list, but gives an idea of the many ways small children develop understanding and ways of behaving:

- watching and copying
- listening
- being shown what to do
- finding that certain things are rewarding
- trying out things and seeing what happens
- doing things with other people
- being asked questions at an appropriate level
- having experiences explained in terms they can understand and in terms of what they already know about the world
- being given the opportunity to practise new skills and knowledge in different situations
- having someone to talk with about what they are doing who will extend their language for thinking and problem-solving.

Infant class teachers use all of the above to teach children the necessary skills that enable them to get along with each other, and to progress within the infant classroom.

Positive reinforcement for wanted behaviours

A very young baby soon discovers that some of her random actions ensure a response from a significant adult – be it a returned smile when she manages a 'windy' smile, a dummy or feed if she cries, and so on. It isn't long before some actions become more deliberate in order to evoke the response required, especially getting attention.

For some young children a simple behaviourist approach is an effective way of increasing wanted behaviours. Pupils are provided with positive reinforcement for those actions that the teacher would like them to learn. The ABC (antecedent/behaviour/consequence) model helps to identify which specific behaviours need to be learned, those factors within a situation which exacerbate difficulties by reinforcing unwanted behaviour and how new learning may be best reinforced.

Taking other factors into account

For most children, however, a social learning perspective offers more possibilities. This takes into account how factors influence each other in a reciprocal way. This includes thoughts and feelings as well as actions and a range of factors within the environment. It moves away from the idea of a simple cause and effect – if you do *this* then *that* will happen, to one which recognises that everything affects everything else. Personal construct theory provides an additional dimension in the focus it has on individual perceptions. Whatever intervention is decided upon, it needs to make sense, not only to the teacher but also to the child.

	Antecedent	Behaviour	Consequence
Problem	Class asked to tidy up	Ali dives under a table shortly followed by Derrick. They then play crawling and chasing games and don't help tidy up.	Teacher gets cross, shouts at both children, hauls them out from under the table or keep them after school to be told off.
Children's response	OH NO!	LOTS OF FUN!	LOTS OF ATTENTION
Solution	Ali and Derrick are told that when they tidy up they will get a well done stamp on their arms to show their mummy. They are asked what bit of tidying up they will do, asked how they will do it – are reminded when asked to tidy up.	Ali and Derrick are prompted by the teacher - they do their bit of tidying . When done they are asked to stand by the teacher to wait for their stamp.	Teacher stamps a special well done mark on their arms.....says......would you like a different colour one tomorrow? Tomorrow she reminds them.
Children's response	OH WELL	THIS ISN'T SO BAD	LOTS OF ATTENTION

Figure 4.2 The antecedent/behaviour/consequence model

New behaviour is learned gradually

Sometimes teachers become despondent because they have thought hard about what a child needs to improve but behaviour doesn't seem to be changing despite their interventions. If this is the case then it might be worth thinking of the steps involved in getting to the desired behaviour and expecting the whole process to take longer as a result.

It may be helpful to use as a more detailed example some very early learning experiences that occur long before a child starts school. This illustrates the way a new behaviour is taught using carefully planned steps, which maximise the success of the venture.

A toddler who is being toilet trained will almost always be trained in stages even if the adult concerned is unaware of the process.
What happens may be along the following lines:

- A potty appears in the household and the child gets used to having this object around the place
- he is encouraged to sit on the potty
- he learns that it is expected that when you sit on the potty you take your pants off
- he is encouraged to sit on the potty at specific times
- when the child 'produces' (which initially is usually by chance), the adult is happy and this is communicated to the child
- this is repeated until the child comes to understand what is expected
- being motivated by the adult's response the child makes an effort to do what is expected.
- the child develops a sense of achievement for himself and relies less on the adult's response
- the behaviour may be reinforced by pretend play and getting teddy to sit on the potty
- once the behaviour is established, the adult's response each time is decreased, and is gradually phased out.

Some parents may initially use an additional motivating factor, such as a small sweet as a reward, and again, this would be gradually phased out.

Most infant teachers will tend to teach required behaviour in a similar way, although some may not consciously analyse what they are doing in such detail. They may also condense certain steps, according to the needs of the children they have at the time.

Fear of failure

If, however, the child experienced reprimands for not performing, then he will associate these times with distress and will try to avoid the situation altogether, perhaps to the frustration of the adult and the failure of the whole operation. Similarly in school if a child is continually told that he can't do something and comes to feel that learning situations are painful then he will avoid making the effort.

Some children need to learn to be motivated. These are two possible approaches to new learning situations:

I know what to do and/or I've been successful before
I expect I will be able do it
I want to try

or

I don't know what to do and/or I've failed before
I probably won't be able do it
I don't want to try

Adult expectations and responses can both help children develop a self-concept as a successful learner or they can undermine confidence. This applies to all learning.

Behaviour can be replaced

Although it is possible to teach small children the behaviour that is desirable in an infant classroom, there may be those who have already learned behaviours that are unhelpful at best and unacceptable at worst. It will be one of the teacher's tasks to ensure that these behaviours are discouraged, and replaced by that which is more acceptable. It may be possible to examine the context in which the behaviour happens, and alter or remove the antecedents that cause the behaviour in future. Sometimes it is not practicable or possible, as the antecedents may be unknown or beyond reach. In this case, we must carefully consider the consequences of the behaviour, not only for that child, but for others. It may be useful if the target behaviour for a child is incompatible with the one that is causing the most difficulty, e.g. focusing on promoting 'on-seat' behaviour rather than using sanctions against 'under the table' behaviour!

Catch the child being 'good'

Attention is a powerful reinforcer. If one of the consequences of a child's unwanted behaviour is that adult attention is focused on that child, then this may unwittingly reinforce the behaviour, and cause it to be repeated. A decision needs to be made about which behaviours can be ignored – usually minor misbehaviours – and which cannot. The principal of not reinforcing poor behaviour used on its own has limited success, as the child may 'step-up' the behaviour until it is not possible to ignore it any longer. What also needs to happen is for the child to get more focused attention from adults when they are exhibiting desired behaviour. In other words, 'Catch them being good'. The more difficulties a child has with one behaviour, the greater the need to focus attention elsewhere. Some teachers respond to these ideas by asking: 'Why should I praise that pupil for doing what the others are doing anyway?' The answer is for a number of reasons:

- the child will get your attention anyway – it is better if it is for something positive
- the child will learn that behaving appropriately will earn adult approval
- other children will become aware that positive behaviours are noticed
- they will also begin to understand that if they copy the good behaviour, they too may get attention.

Be specific

Blanket comments such as 'Good' or 'Well done' have limited usefulness, as they may have little meaning for children – we have all heard pupils promise to 'be good' without having the slightest understanding of what that entails. It is far better to comment specifically :

'Thank you for sitting nicely.'
'I can see that you've been very kind to ....'
'This table has worked hard to tidy away the crayons etc.'

This will then reinforce all the expectations that a teacher has.

Consequences

Not all behaviours can be ignored, especially those that are unsafe. In some cases, children need to learn that some behaviours have negative consequences for them. A consequence is different from a punishment in that it:

- is planned and not erratic
- is offered calmly to the child as a choice
- is linked as closely as possible to the behaviour.

One of the most effective negative consequences is removal from the group for a period of time, usually a matter of minutes. The child needs to know exactly why his behaviour is unacceptable but if the child becomes calm, rejoining the group needs to take place without comment or reference to the offence. If used consistently this strategy can be highly effective. Some teachers use a chair a little apart from the group, others a special cushion for the pupil to sit on. For some pupils, merely missing a turn is sufficient.

Any discussion with the child, or reprimand, should be carried out as soon as possible afterwards and without an audience. It is also helpful if the teacher quickly identifies an opportunity for a positive comment to that child which reinforces expected behaviour. This also re-establishes a positive teacher/child interaction.

Reminders before reprimands

Some children with special learning needs are given guidance before a lesson so that they can understand better what to do. The same principle is effective for behaviour. Prompting and reminding pupils quietly, possibly offering them the opportunity to be models for others, can increase both their skills and their self-esteem. When children are not conforming, reminding pupils first may negate the need for reprimands.

Making sense to the child

Teachers know why they are teaching certain kinds of behaviour, certain routines etc, but to many of the children in an infant class, the reasons are not apparent, or beyond their current comprehension. Compliance in learning to behave as expected must therefore have some rationale or payoff for the individuals concerned. As well as being clearly explained in ways which promote 'fairness' it is useful if children have good feelings when they comply. As most children want to please, a smile, wink, nod or thumbs-up sign from the teacher that shows they have been noticed is often sufficient – or a small reward like being given a sticker or allowed to do a special job like taking the register to the office – a process remarkably similar to that used in the potty training!

Some pupils will not need any adult reinforcement in order to learn new behaviour particularly if they find the task itself rewarding or interesting, or if they are self-confident, with a strong sense of self-esteem. They will, however, still bask in the attention that they get when teacher is pleased with them. There are a few pupils who will not manage to respond much to teacher direction initially and appear to 'lose face' when forced to comply. This is likely to be the result of prolonged negative interaction with battles to determine who has had the upper hand. These pupils may already have learned that to comply is to lose. Any confrontation with these pupils is likely to escalate, and a better approach is to leave them with a good idea of what is expected, and then move away or leave them with some small amount of choice – e.g. the order in which things are to be done. With a calm but assertive approach which leaves some way for the child to make a limited choice, thereby having some control, many of these pupils will respond.

Working in the 'tomorrow' of the child

The phrase 'zone of proximal development' was coined by the Russian psychologist Vygotsky who wanted to convey the need to target teaching at an appropriate level for the individual child. This is where learning is achievable for the child but also presents challenges. Vygotsky defines the ZPD as being the difference between the level of tasks that can be achieved with adult (or peer) guidance and help and the level at which they can be performed independently. This emphasises the importance and power of instruction and building on what the child knows now. In Vygotsky's model the child is likely to learn more effectively when interacting with peers who are more competent and who can both provide models for the child to copy and help to mediate meaning. Teachers need also to 'scaffold' experiences for the child so that he is able to achieve success.

Although Vygotsky was focusing on cognitive learning these aspects of his theories provide perspectives on social learning which teachers may wish to take into account when planning behavioural intervention. Some schools, for instance, have found that having greater flexibility between classes both gives older children the chance to show what they know and younger children the chance to learn from other children.

Learning new ways of understanding

Often a teacher may feel that a child needs to learn to think about themselves and/or situations differently in order to behave more appropriately. A learning target may therefore be to encourage a more positive self-concept or promote some problem-solving skills which enable the child to develop new ways of seeing things. The teaching approach would be to structure situations and opportunities in which new 'labels' could be introduced and reinforced. The child could be encouraged to think about how these new ideas about herself might apply to many situations. The perspectives of other pupils also need to be taken into account.

A child who overreacts, for instance, to situations in which she feels rejected may need to learn the following:

- that she is a full and valuable member of the class group
- that it is important to others that she is there
- ways of joining groups positively
- acceptable ways of expressing distress.

Other children also need to learn to recognise her developing skills and respond accordingly.

A teaching approach could be a strong focus over a given time on these targets which permeate curricular activities, peer group collaboration, social activities, direct training and role play in small groups, carpet and circle time sessions and whole class development. This will not only meet the child's needs but develop many skills and positive perspectives for others in the class.

Summary

There are many different ways to view children's behaviour, some of which lead to a sense of helplessness and others which are far more empowering. Teachers have the best chance of success in managing behaviour by looking at what children need to learn, and what needs to be taken into consideration in promoting that learning. Giving consideration to the ways in which the whole class learn appropriate behaviour for school is the first step. As with other special needs, children who find it more difficult to behave well need a more structured approach, which takes into account how they think and feel about themselves and what is expected of them.

Checklist for teaching behaviour

1. What does the child need to learn? What are you aiming for?

2. Where is the child now in relation to your target?

3. What is the first step(s) towards this?

4. What are you going to do to teach her?

5. What teaching approaches will you use?

6. What factors in the environment are part of the plan?
   - Peers, parents, other people
   - Expectations, opportunities
   - Classroom layout, reinforcers etc

7. What factors for the child do you need to take into account?
   - Strengths, personality, level of understanding, language skills
   - Self-concept, self-esteem, emotional fragility
   - Physical needs, anxieties, tiredness etc.

8. Does your learning target make sense to the child?
   What is the 'pay-off' for her?

9. How will you ensure that the child experiences success?

10. What do you need to support your intervention?

11. Do you still think what you are aiming for is appropriate or would another learning target or approach be better?

12. How will you know that the child is making progress?

CHAPTER 5

THE NEEDS OF TEACHERS

The happiness and progress of children as they pass through the educational system is the result of many interrelated factors. The quality of learning, however, will be heavily influenced by the attitude, commitment and expertise of teachers. The role of the infant class teacher is particularly complex, and those who teach very young children don't always appreciate the range of skills that they use during an average day. Teachers are more likely to be successful in enabling the children in their class to make maximum academic and social progress if they themselves enjoy what they are doing, tend to their own needs, and have a sense of job satisfaction. This chapter clarifies the needs that teachers have and suggests ways in which these might be met.

What it takes

Teachers are more likely to enjoy their work if:

- they feel comfortable in their knowledge of what they have to teach and ways in which to teach it, of their pupils and of the procedures and routines within the school;
- they feel confident in their own ability to manage the class and are able to maintain high self-esteem;
- they are able to manage their time effectively and are not totally exhausted at the end of every day;
- they have some control over their immediate environment and can make it work for them;
- they feel valued and supported by the school and community in which they work, and do not feel isolated.

Factual information needed by teachers

Apart from knowledge of the curriculum and teaching methods, teachers require additional information which will enable them to meet the needs of the children in their class. This will come from a variety of sources and includes:

- Information about pupils: much of this will come from meetings with parents prior to their child starting school, or in the case of particular children, from other professionals such as speech therapists, social workers or educational psychologists. Some of the information could be of a sensitive nature, and issues of confidentiality will need to be considered. Teachers should know where files are kept, who has access to them and what and how the information given relates to their work.

- School and LEA policies on Special Needs, Behaviour, Attendance, Equal Opportunities, Child Protection and Health and Safety. Teachers need to check school procedures to clarify their role and responsibility in the implementation of such policies.
- Referral routes to other agencies and professionals. Teachers need to know when a referral is appropriate and who is the named person in the school with responsibility for linking with each of these agencies. In many schools access to services is via the SENCO or deputy head. It is also important to know when it is appropriate to pass problems onto the more senior members of staff, rather than class teachers taking responsibility.
- Arrangements about contact with parents, who will do what and when. (See also Chapter 6, 'The Needs of Parents')

Having confidence

Whatever training or experience a teacher has had, it is probably true that much of their classroom practice has been learnt on the job. Each change of school or class brings new learning opportunities as well as challenges. There may be times when teachers feel that they have less skills or knowledge than they need. Together with all of the daily pressures in school this can lead to teachers doubting their own ability. When teachers start to feel that they are not capable of the demands of the job, this damages their self-esteem. The end result is teacher stress and further feelings of being deskilled.

Accepting limits

The 'perfect' teacher does not exist. Accepting that there will be situations that require help is not an admission of failure. There may be members of staff with exactly the necessary expertise for the situation causing concern. It is important to recognise when it is appropriate to share problems and concerns with other, or more senior members of staff, rather than try to deal with them entirely alone.

Making mistakes is normal and we can learn from them. The teacher who acknowledges her errors to the class is giving children the message that making mistakes is part of the learning process and is modelling a useful response. Saying sorry, perhaps for overreacting or for being tired and snappy, tends to win rather than undermine respect. Small children can often show remarkable tolerance and understanding in such circumstances!

Teachers cannot be expected to be able to do everything that is asked of them on the spot. They need to decide which can be done now and which can be left until later. There will be things for which a teacher is not the most appropriate person to take responsibility and where there are doubts this should be checked up on. Some child protection issues may come into this category.

From time to time, it is a great boost to revisit things that have been achieved. Making a 'positive feedback file' where successes can be noted is as useful for teachers as it is for pupils in maintaining self-esteem.

Looking after yourself

No-one has a bottomless pot of either emotional or physical energy. Sometimes it needs re-filling rather than draining. It is not sensible to give endlessly to others at the expense of your own personal needs. Teachers will find it an increasing struggle to meet the needs of the children in their class if their own needs are unmet. These are some ways in which teachers can attend to their own needs:

- Caring for health to maximise energy levels must be a priority. People who eat healthily, have enough sleep and find time to relax won't burn themselves out and have a better chance of being effective in the classroom.
- Mental health is as important as physical health. People need to give themselves permission to STOP sometimes. Stress relievers such as spending time with friends, physical exercise, meditation, yoga, massage and holidays all have their place.
- Feeling in control increases confidence. This can apply equally to the classroom environment, to daily planning, or to promoting positive behaviours. To be in control entails being prepared in advance for what might happen.

    One interpretation of this is having work set aside that the children can do if you are absent from school. It also includes having a classroom discipline plan so that when a child behaves in a certain way, both you and the pupils will know what will happen as a consequence. This means you can be consistent, and won't have to think 'on the spot' – often when emotions are running high. This can help reduce anxiety .
- Keeping up to date with recent educational developments, even skimming through professional publications, can raise confidence. This might include persuading the school to subscribe to such publications that

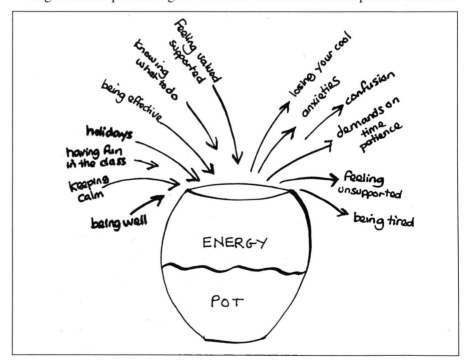

Figure 5.1 Keep a balance

are then available to everyone in the staff room. Seeking out opportunities for further professional training also helps.

- Having fun with the class can be a great tension reliever. Doing things occasionally which are a treat for everyone and structuring situations where the class all laughs together can lift the spirits of both pupils and teacher. A sense of humour used appropriately, can help develop a group identity, as well as deflect potentially difficult situations.
- Developing a non-work related interest outside of school hours can be an integral part of looking after yourself.
- Teachers whose lives outside work are particularly stressful should seriously consider whether counselling might help them to cope.

Managing time

Almost every infant teacher says that there isn't enough time. Although time is finite, careful planning will make its use more effective, and the teacher less stressed. Planning involves goal setting for pupils, but should also include the setting of goals for teachers. These must be realistic and not too numerous to ensure they are achieved. This leads to a feeling of success and of being in control. Planning however should always take account of the need for flexibility, so that if anything changes there is space for adjustment.

Successful time management, and the minimising of teacher stress can be helped by the following:

- ☞ Careful planning for the short, medium, and long term. Prioritising and distributing time may mean organising a timetable for yourself, and adhering to it. This could include timetabling for preparation, staff meetings, liaison with parents/other professionals, planning, setting up displays, and all of the myriad tasks that are part of the life of a teacher.
- ☞ Keeping a list and crossing off the things that have been completed.
- ☞ Breaking down larger tasks into smaller ones that can be managed in smaller chunks of time.
- ☞ Arriving early enough in the day to get some of the organisational tasks done without disturbance.
- ☞ Thinking carefully about the roles of other adults who may be in the classroom, such as the welfare assistant or nursery nurse and delegating work accordingly.
- ☞ Organising parent helpers to do some of the routine tasks on a regular basis.
- ☞ It is helpful to close up areas of the room one by one as they are tidied,

Figure 5.2 Tasks for the day

so that the teacher does not have to do this once the pupils have left at the end of the day.

The classroom environment

Many teachers work in deprived areas in schools that are in a poor state of repair. At times, these factors may be a source of stress. Within certain physical constraints, however, the immediate environment of the classroom is within the teacher's sphere of influence and there are distinct advantages to be had by giving careful thought to the layout and appearance of their classroom. These benefits include an environment that:

- is comfortable and convenient for both teachers and children to work in
- promotes positive behaviour by minimising situations that may engender conflict and disruption.

It is worth giving thought to the following:

☛ A classroom that is pleasant to be in and reflects the teacher's taste and values will be one that the teacher will want to return to everyday. Personal touches will make the classroom more pleasant for pupils too. They can be involved in discussions about any changes that may be made, and learn about taking responsibility for the environment on an immediate and personal level.

☛ Warm and soothing colours can have a calming effect in the classroom. Although children like primary colours, and bright, busy classrooms may be appealing to many adults, they may also be over-stimulating for pupils, especially those who have trouble focusing on one thing at a time.

☛ Positioning specific activity areas with care. Teachers will need to be able to quickly move to areas where free choice, noisy, or physical activities are taking place. Easy access will minimise wasted time and teacher stress. There also needs to be free passage for visitors to the classroom, and for message-bearers. Obviously, messy activities and materials needed for them, such as painting, water play etc. should be located as near the sink as is practicable.

☛ Consideration to the location of frequently needed equipment. Children can be gradually trained to get things for themselves and this will free teacher time as well as delegating responsibility to groups or individuals. The use of containers that are easily identified and labelled with words and pictures will encourage children to put things away without adult help.

☛ consideration to the location of the teacher's workstation (if there is one) so that it is possible to scan the classroom to spot potential difficulties before they become critical. Having particular pupils and noisy activities in a direct line of vision at all times is helpful.

☛ Some children will have needs which require special consideration as to where they sit in the classroom e.g. some may need to be near to the toilets, others may be helped by being seated where they are less distracted by other pupils or by what is going on in the playground. Classroom furniture can be carefully arranged to section off parts of the room.

☛ Positioning any areas where quiet activities take place away from noisier ones; this will minimise distraction for those pupils in the quiet area.

☛ Limiting the number of children that can participate in an activity, particularly where there are safety issues, can be helpful.

☛ Consideration needs to be given to the delivery of directions to the class. When the teacher is talking, will some pupils be out of sight, whilst others may have to twist in their seats? This may have quite serious implications in terms of pupil compliance. On the other hand it might be more appropriate for all directions to be given when pupils are seated on the carpet and the teacher alongside.

The 'network of support'

In-school

All teachers have different levels of tolerance and frustration. What is 'unmanageable' to one individual may be merely 'a bit of a headache' to another. This same teacher may find a different behaviour is the one that really gets to her, making her grit her teeth and count to ten. These levels fluctuate for each individual teacher depending on what else is going on in their lives. The 'what else' can include what is going on at home, physical and mental health factors, the pressures of the curriculum, the number of children in the class and most especially how the teacher feels about the support and understanding she receives from colleagues and the overall ethos of the school. A school that is accepting of and positive towards children is more likely to have an ethos that is concerned for the welfare of its staff also. Children who are angry and distressed are likely to have teachers who feel that way too after a while. If children are unable to settle to learning, use bad language, are aggressive to other, gentler children and defiantly disobedient when asked to do something, it is unsurprising that they undermine the ability of teachers to do their job and threaten their self-esteem. It is easy at this point to forget how little, vulnerable and needy such children are. Teachers need to be patient.

No teacher should have to feel that she dreads the day ahead because of one child. Neither should she feel that she is unsupported in this situation.

Sharing responsibility

The teacher's first ally could be any colleague with whom she feels comfortable but the school's special needs co-ordinator is particularly well placed to share her concerns and discuss possible strategies for management. The school's behaviour management policy should be a constant source of reference so that practice and policy are cohesive and the ethos of the school reinforced. For entrenched difficulties the whole staff will need to discuss the approach that will be used so that there is clarity and consistency.

The following are some ways that have helped to involve other members of staff, in a positive way, to provide support or at times, relief from a difficult pupil.

☛ Occasionally it may be really useful for an 'observer' that the teacher is comfortable with to spend some time in the classroom in order to suggest possible ways of intervening.
☛ The class can be taken by another member of staff, to release the teacher to carry out her own observations or some direct work with an individual child. If this is a pattern of working within the school which is used by more experienced members of staff as well as those newer to the profes-

sion, then it is more likely to be seen as supportive rather than threatening.

☞ Some pupils need time-out to avoid attention for negative behaviour. Sending them to the class of a colleague to work and calm down can be a very useful strategy. This can be particularly successful when the pupil receives minimal attention from adults and peers. Providing it is not used too frequently, a reciprocal arrangement with another teacher in the school can be useful both for the management of difficult behaviour and as a source of mutual support.

☞ If the school also supports some flexibility of approach it makes it easier to share responsibility in a real way. For example, one school arranged for a child in Year 2 who appeared to have behaviour difficulties linked to difficulties with learning, to spend three afternoons a week in the nursery. This has enabled a clearer identification of his level of abilities, provided him with some positive school experiences in which he could be successful and given the class teacher a necessary break.

☞ Some schools have set up problem solving groups which meet regularly to focus on a problem or pupil brought by a member of staff. These can be very effective in allowing different perspectives to be considered, and work well, provided that the ground rules of such a group are clear and the ethos of the school is supportive. Similar support groups may also be set up between a small number of local schools: here there are meetings once or twice a term to problem-solve.

Throughout this book there is a strong emphasis on working with parents. The better the 'working relationship' between home and school the more that teachers will feel that the responsibility for changing a child's behaviour is shared.

Sharing feelings

It is also important to identify the emotional support that may be required. At a basic level this means someone who will just listen when things have been really bad. A sensitive listener may also help the teacher to see how certain aspects of a child's behaviour may be touching on their particular vulnerabilities. It is a short step from this to thinking about ways in which it may be possible to distance oneself emotionally and not take matters so personally. It is more helpful to focus on this rather than to collude with a perspective which reinforces labels for the child and attributes blame. Although it may be hard to give and receive, there needs to be encouragement and reassurance sometimes even for the most able and experienced of teachers.

Support from outside agencies

Referral to outside agencies happens at Stage Three of the Code of Practice. Where concerns have been carefully identified in school and individual education programmes planned, carried out and reviewed this will also help in deciding what it is that outside agencies can best offer to the situation. Sometimes this will be a more specialist assessment but often teachers are simply seeking new ways of thinking about a problem. Educational psychologists, behaviour support teachers or other agencies do not themselves have magic wands and are there to support the school's efforts rather than come up with answers which will make the problems disappear. New perspectives on difficulties are useful in devising ways forward and having input from someone who is skilled at finding out what sense the child is making of the situation can be valuable in deciding how best to begin to address the difficulties. When anxieties and/or exasperation levels are high it is often tempting to believe that an extra person in the classroom would be the answer. Sometimes this really is going to be the case but it should be clear what that person is needed to do. When resources in the form of additional 'hands-on' support are required, the role of a support teacher or assistant does need to be thought through at the outset with clarity about expectations. Consideration need to be given to the length of time an additional person will be required and what the criteria will be for reducing the support or moving to another Stage. Regular meetings to monitor how this is working also need to be built in to initial planning.

Summary

Teachers' needs must be taken into consideration when thinking about promoting a positive ethos within a class. These needs are both cognitive, for information and skill development, and affective, to feel confident and supported. Teachers, like anyone else, need to predominantly enjoy their job and achieve a sense of professional satisfaction in what they do. Teachers can only be fully effective in the classroom when they have a high level of self-esteem, manage both their time and their energies in a planned and balanced way and feel some collegiality with colleagues.

CHAPTER 6

THE NEEDS OF PARENTS

Previous chapters have illustrated some of the differences in terms of developmental level, and access to social and learning experiences, that may exist within any one group of children starting school for the first time. Their parents too, will be a similarly heterogeneous group and will have a range of expectations and experiences. They will also have different demands on them which may include other children in the family, work pressures, social and financial considerations or domestic difficulties. Their needs, however, like the needs of children, will have many similarities.

This chapter looks at what parents might need in order to maximise their willingness and ability to be 'partners' with teachers in promoting both learning and positive behaviour.

First impressions

The focus of most books on education is naturally on the needs of children and of their teachers. It is, however, essential that the needs of parents are also acknowledged and understood, particularly in these early years. The first experiences that parents have when they enter their child's new school can promote or damage relationships for the future.

When we are talking about the behaviour of young children, we *must* include parents if we hope to move forward positively. It is easy for people to feel threatened and defensive, devalued and deskilled, blamed and guilty. None of this is helpful and schools need to think through approaches which will foster mutual collaboration and understanding. When the foundation stones for this are put in place early on it is much easier to work together to solve the problems that may arise later.

Messages are passed to parents in a variety of ways, not only through the formal channels where factual information is communicated, but also in unspoken or less obvious ways. The ethos of a school is very powerful in determining whether parents feel comfortable and confident in communicating with staff and collaborating with teachers' efforts for their children.

The need to feel confident

Parents need to know that their child is safe

More than anything else, parents need to feel secure that their child is safe in school. This can no longer be a given in any circumstances. After recent tragic incidents, parents may very well be highly anxious about leaving their

Figure 6.1 Classroom poster celebrating diversity of languages

children. A 'barbed wire' mentality, however, is also not conducive to a school that is welcoming to parents and security measures have to be seen in the light of this. Parents can be reassured by knowing that the school has thought through the following aspects of child safety and can answer their questions:

- the physical arrangements which stop children running out of school and strangers coming in
- the supervision arrangements which ensure that someone will always know where their child is
- behaviour policies which include a whole school code of conduct which applies to both staff and pupils.

The behaviour of some children is often a concern to other parents who may be worried that their own child will be the target of aggression. It is particularly difficult for schools to address this sensitively and keep a balance between the needs of the individual and the safety of others. When parents are fully informed at the outset about how the school addresses social and behavioural issues and the rationale behind this, then they are more likely to be supportive rather than condemnatory when difficult situations arise.

When some children first go to school this may be the first time they have spent any time away from their parents. Usually this is taken into consideration when settling them into school life. The significance of this first separation for parents, however, also needs to be acknowledged. Handing over a precious child into the hands of another adult for the first time can be very daunting and at the very least may be the cause of some anxiety. This 'loss' for parents may be communicated to children, and cause them anxiety in turn. Other parents, perhaps those who also have younger children, may leave their child with a sense of relief. It helps if teachers show that they recognise all these feelings as valid and understandable.

Parents need to know that their child is learning

Parents need to feel confident that their child will learn in school. Parents who have perhaps had little formal education or whose schooling has taken place in other countries and cultures or who have had little or no experience in the setting into which their own children are now being placed, may bring with them assumptions and beliefs about what goes on in school. They have views about what should be happening which are not necessarily reflected in their child's experiences in school. They may worry that their son or daughter should be doing certain things or in a certain way and not be doing some of the activities that do take place. Other parents will be aware from the media about recent changes in education and may be apprehensive about the implications of these changes for their children. These same parents may feel themselves to be 'out of touch', and unable to help their children without appearing foolish or uncaring.

It is important that the purpose of classroom activities is communicated to all parents so that they can understand how each fits in with the early years curriculum. They also need good information about how they can help and support their children. This needs to be available in the languages of the community.

☛ Some schools have made a short video to show parents what goes on in the classroom and why and have found this very helpful. Parents are particularly motivated to come and see a film, shown during the year when their own child is one of the stars!

The need to feel valued

There are those parents whose own experiences of school were not particularly happy and who felt unsuccessful and devalued. It is possible that they feel that teachers did not treat them well. When their own children start school these uncomfortable feelings are brought to the fore and going through the school gates might be difficult as it revives painful memories. Parents need to feel comfortable and welcome on the school premises. What they have to say and offer should be seen as important. This is particularly true of parents who may feel that negative judgements will be made about them and either take a defensive stance or lack the confidence to express fears or worries.

Communication with teachers.

Good relationships may go wrong at a very early stage if parents are unclear about when it is appropriate to speak to their child's teacher. Coming into the classroom to try and explain a difficulty while the teacher is fully occupied with the children can make the teacher feel irritated and the parent feel that she is at best not being listened to and at worst ignored. Whatever arrangements are in place about the start of the school day, whether parents

Figure 6.2 First day at school. What was it like for them?

can stay with their child as long as they wish, or are expected to leave their child at ten past nine, should be made clear at the outset. There also needs to be a system in place for parents to relay to the class teacher any information that she needs to know on that day, sometimes privately. Other discussions should be taking place at an arranged time when teachers have made themselves available. Some schools have done away with a formal 'parents evening' but see several parents/carers one late afternoon a week on a rota system. Some teachers leave the first twenty minutes after the end of each school day for any parent who wants to have a word about their child. Details about when parents are welcome to talk to teachers and when not should be advertised clearly and permanently for each class.

☛ A clipboard and pen left at the entrance to the classroom can enable a parent to communicate simple, non-confidential information to the teacher. A wipe-board is even better. Another can be used for communication from the teacher to the parent. However, consideration does need to be given to the parent who is not literate, or not literate in English.

☛ Some teachers circulate in the playground, or wherever parents congregate at the start of the day, for the first fifteen minutes prior to the school sessions starting.

A parent/carers room

Many schools have established and appreciated the benefits of a parents/carers room. It is not always easy to allocate valuable space, but having a room where parents, particularly those with younger children, can meet together is welcomed by many parents. The room should be easily accessible and efforts made to keep it tidy and clean and well cared for. Some parents may be prepared to do this on a rota. It should contain facilities to make a drink and sit comfortably and toys and books to occupy younger children. Articles and relevant school or local authority and community information can be made available. Specific requests for help in school could be written on the noticeboard. Again, consideration needs to be given to the community languages of parents, and the inclusion of those parents whose first language is not English, as well as those from different cultures.

Figure 6.3 Information for parents

This can provide a venue useful for the establishment of good parent-parent relationships and will also provide a base for the parents of children who take longer to settle at school initially. The parent can then withdraw from the child, yet be available on the premises, until the child becomes more at ease in the classroom.

The need to feel skilled

Parents have many skills, and there are many opportunities for involving them in the life of the school, apart from the usual fund-raising. Opportunities need to be made clear for those parents who are willing, and have the time, to become more involved in the school. Parents can be involved in working with small groups, e.g. sports, cooking activities, hearing children read – all under the guidance of the class teacher, as well as participating in class outings. Some schools have tapped into other areas and have invited parents (and grandparents) to come into school to talk about their work, experiences or interests.

☞ One local school has asked several parents to come and talk to children about some of the things they do. Parents who initially responded were

53

LIVERPOOL HOPE UNIVERSITY COLLEGE

a doctor, a fire-fighter, and someone who brought his rock collection to school. His enthusiasm and knowledge about this transfixed the class. A grandmother was asked to come and talk to a few children about what it is was like to live in the area many years ago. Another school asked several Bangladeshi parents if they would tell the school about any songs and rhymes that were familiar to pre-school children so that these could be included in 'carpet time activities' or in the playground.

The above is a good use of a valuable resource. Such an input, and the work resulting from it, is able to address several attainment targets in the National Curriculum.

Some parents may feel hesitant about offering any help because they feel that it will be a regular and possibly onerous commitment. Some may feel that they don't 'fit in' with the cohort of parents who are involved on a regular basis. A personal approach for a one-off involvement in the school which highlights a particular skill will do much to make that parent feel valued as a contributor, especially if a formal note of thanks follows.

There are times that a school really does need a parent to be more involved, when for example concern is expressed about their own child. The difference between parents supporting the school generally and supporting efforts to help their own child, needs to be made clear.

When discussing a child who has a problem with behaviour, parents may feel that their skills as a parent are being called into question. Parents should always be asked what is realistically possible for them to do to support the school's endeavours and how any strategy fits in with other demands on them.

The need to have other concerns acknowledged

Seeing parental participation as something that the school values can have many benefits for the children and encourages a sense of community. There needs to be an awareness, however, that not all families will be able, or want, to be this involved. It's a fine line between encouragement and pressure and it is not helpful if parents feel guilty that they are not doing as much as others to support the school. Parents need to feel that the school takes account of those aspects of their own lives and that they are supported in their difficulties and endeavours and not condemned if they do not meet the school's requests for help. Some may have the demands of other children or older relatives to cope with, some might be welcoming the opportunity to gain some personal freedom, return to work or embark on a college course. There are those parents who may be overwhelmed with situations which are not easy to talk about such as family breakdown, ill health or financial difficulties. If good relationships and communication are established at the outset within a supportive framework it will be easier for parents to talk about those things which may very well be affecting their child's ability to learn and behave in school.

Some families will not have had sufficient educational experiences to become fully literate themselves. This may be a source of embarrassment, especially when they are asked to support reading at home. Sometimes teachers are not aware of such difficulties and may view lack of parental response as lack of interest. A school which makes it possible for parents to communicate their own difficulties will not only be able to direct parents to sources of help should they want this, but also be helping the children by exploring alternative means of support.

What parents need to know when their children start school

Initial communication to parents needs to deal with:

- who will be responsible for the care of their child
- what the security arrangements are
- what the routines of the school day are
- how parents can help to ensure that children are prepared for each day e.g. with reading book, PE kit
- the importance of a good night's sleep and something to eat before school
- making clear what will happen in the classroom and why
- the school policy on behaviour and its rationale
- how parents can continue to develop positive behaviours at home
- the role of structured play in helping children learn
- how important parents are as participants in the education of their children – especially talking to them, showing interest in what they do and being positive about every small success and every effort.

Essential information connected with the above could include the following:

- the timing of the school day
- lunch time arrangements
- expectations about clothing
- materials/equipment/money needed for various activities
- school policies e.g. Reading, Behaviour, Special Needs etc.
- National Curriculum & SATS
- home-school communications
- parent-teacher links
- when teachers are available to parents both on an informal and a formal basis
- opportunities for parents to help in school
- how they can support their child's learning at home
- arrangements that the school will make if children are not collected within a certain time at the end of the day, or are absent for an unexplained period of time.

How information is communicated

Attention needs to be paid to the ways in which essential information is given out. Some of this is straightforward and factual, e.g. the timing of the school day, whilst other information such as expectations of behaviour and School Policies, for example, may need further explanation, and the opportunity for parents to ask questions.

Prior to the new intake starting at school, most schools have at least one meeting to give out information to in-coming parents. Some schools have several such meetings, often at different times of the day, each with a slightly different focus. The purpose of one such meeting might be to enable parents to meet other adults connected to the school with whom their child might come into contact, such as nursery assistants, the school meals midday supervisors, secretary and caretaker. School governors, especially the parent governors, could also be invited to these meetings. Parents as well as children, feel reassured if they can put a face to the name.

If class lists are available, parents could also be introduced to each other. This may be helpful later on in the establishment of:

- friendships between children
- contact between parents.

The latter is important particularly for first-time parents, those new to the area, or those in accommodation which does not readily facilitate social contact. When parents have the opportunity to get to know one another, they can develop ways of mutual support, such as sharing taking the children to and from school. Good friendships established between parents at this time in their child's life can last for years and prove to be of invaluable support for parents, as well as a source of pleasure for both parents and children. It also creates an informal information network.

Whatever arrangements for liaison with the parents of in-coming reception children, and the number of meetings that this may entail, there will be quite a lot of information to disseminate. This information is essential, but it isn't always possible for parents to digest it in one go. In the words of one teacher: 'Everything we talk about, we put on paper'. This might seem extravagant in terms of photocopying, but it saves time and effort later.

A copy of the most recent newsletter can be placed in a prominent position within the school, such as on the main door. This can be a timely reminder when parents are at the school.

Schools will, however, make decisions about the quantity and type of information that is given to parents, and consideration needs to be given to the avoidance of jargon and the provision of translation where necessary. Schools will need to elicit what access is possible to interpreters/translation facilities other than through other parents or teachers. In some circumstances the use of parents or colleagues might not be appropriate

Many schools try to ensure that there is some translation or interpretation of their information into the main community languages of the population that they serve. Communication is a two way process and consideration also needs to be given to the gathering of information from parents about their children.

There also needs to be some mechanism which ensures that this essential information reaches those parents who may bring their children to school after the beginning of the term, either because they have just moved into the area, or because they did not register their children in time.

Summary

The establishment of positive links with parents at the outset of a child's school life is important for many reasons, and can make a great deal of difference to how well a child settles and learns. The more parents understand about what a school is trying to do, and why this is the case, the better they will be able to support and reinforce learning at home, both socially and academically, and the more consistent will be the message to the child.

Communication with parents happens anyway – the difference is in what is communicated and how it is communicated. Schools which have a very positive approach to parents and make strenuous efforts to value their potential contribution as well as understanding the difficulties they may face, have a much better chance of working collaboratively when children present difficulties.

FRAMEWORK FOR AN INITIAL INTERVIEW WITH A PARENT/CARER

The aims

Know what the aims of the interview are, for example:

- to establish a good working relationship between home and school
- to share mutual concerns
- to share ideas and strategies for improving matters
- to develop closer communication
- to throw light on the difficulties the child is experiencing
- to find out whether referrals have been made elsewhere
- to focus on meeting the needs of the child in question (not the other 30 in the class).

The initial approach

When parents are used to coming to school to hear positive things said about their children they are much more willing to come when there are difficulties to discuss. It may be better if difficulties can first be raised in a chat in the usual way but a separate and more private interview may be more appropriate. An initial approach to see a parent is better done verbally and in a way that does not raise anxieties. Formal letters can be quite intimidating. The class teacher should make an informal arrangement with the parent e.g.: 'I've got a few concerns about Danny and I'd like to talk them over with you. I can't really talk now, I'm supposed to be teaching soon. When would be a good time for you?'. This initial meeting should be between the teacher and the parent only.

If the parent has difficulties with the English language they may like to bring someone with them to help interpret or purely for support.

The setting

When the parent comes for the arranged time it is helpful to have the following:

- no-one else in the room
- chairs arranged so that the teacher is not behind a desk
- someone to keep an eye on younger children – or at least some toys to keep them amused
- a notice on the door so you will not be disturbed
- any telephone off the hook.

The process of the discussion

Clarify the time available. Start off by saying how long you have got for this meeting and ask if that is OK with the parent.

- Say something positive about the child in question. This is very important, it will enable the parent to listen to what is being said.
- Ask the parent for their views, e.g.: 'Gina seems a bit upset at the moment. I wonder if you have noticed anything at home or if you know of anything that might be bothering her.'
- Focus on the child's needs, not the child's misdemeanours, e.g. 'I've been worried about Robert for a while – he seems to be having a struggle to make friends/get down to his work'.
- Ask what the parent has done which they have found has helped, e.g.: 'What makes Marlon sit down for more than ten minutes?'
- Find out whether there are any medical concerns, e.g.: 'Have you had his hearing/sight checked lately?'
- Enquire about changed circumstances at home. This may be a sensitive question, parents may not necessarily tell you about difficulties at a first meeting, but if they feel comfortable this time they may confide later.
- Decide on what happens next, for example:

- keep an eye on him
- take her to the health clinic
- give him lots of praise for sharing
- get better information e.g. observe what is actually going on in the playground for a week or two.

It is important that brief notes of the meeting are kept regarding the issues discussed, and agreed action. These need to be filed appropriately.

The follow up

Arrange a follow up meeting. This is essential: a promising initial meeting with clear plans and actions should be followed by a review so that everyone knows what has happened, what actions were successful and what information might have come to light since. It also helps ensure that what was agreed upon gets done. Even if the child is now behaving impeccably, positive feedback, congratulations and thanks to everyone for their efforts add to the overall ethos of the school. If difficulties remain then this provides an opportunity to think about the next step. When both teachers and parents know that a follow up meeting will happen it will help to maintain the consistency of any action. It is also reassuring to parents when they are kept fully informed.

CHAPTER 7

THE NEEDS OF CHILDREN

Children have wide-ranging and complex needs and many books have been written about what these are and how they can or should be met. Here we look briefly at what a child needs in order to learn and thrive in the infant classroom. We have found Maslow's Hierarchy of Human Needs useful as a framework. It illustrates clearly that there are some needs that will be of greater immediacy for some children at certain times and that a teacher who is not aware of this may be less successful in her attempts to focus on other 'higher' needs.

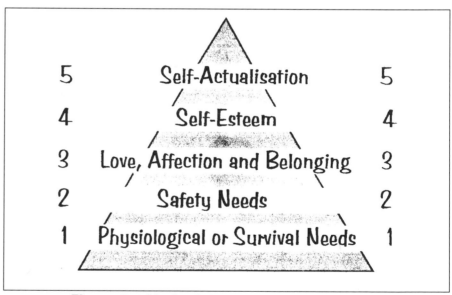

Figure 7.1 Maslow's Hierarchy of Human Needs

Survival needs

Physical survival is the primary need in Maslow's hierarchy. This means the requirement for food, sleep, and adequate shelter. Where there are children in school who are not having these basic needs met then their ability to settle down and learn will be severely diminished. There are some schools, both special and mainstream, who have recognised that offering children something to eat and drink when they arrive in the morning provides for both basic physical nourishment and the need to feel nurtured. Learning is both emotionally and physically tiring. Children need a good night's sleep to function well. When five year olds watch television with their parents until late evening or are kept awake by anxiety, it isn't surprising that they are tired, irritable and unable to learn and behave well in school the next day.

Safety needs

Children need to feel that school is a safe place to be, that people there will look after them and that others will not be allowed to bully or intimidate. For some children where life has already proved to be a risky business, school may be the first place in which they experience some real security. Teachers who are calm and reassuring and provide an ordered, consistent environment increase children's ability to see that some things in the world can be predictable and reliable. This in turn increases their feelings of safety in school. Where there is a high level of unpredictability and insecurity at home children will bring their fears with them and may find it impossible not to keep thinking of events which are worrying. These intrusive thoughts may provoke unexpected behaviours for which the child is unable to articulate reasons.

The need for clear boundaries

Children cannot feel secure and safe if the adults who are caring for them do not provide boundaries. Young children do not have the knowledge, skills or confidence to cope with unlimited freedom and although the drive for independence means that they will push limits in many directions they need to know that the limits are there. Small children are only at the early stages of establishing their own boundaries and it is therefore imperative that responsible adults make it very clear what they can and cannot do, what will keep them (and others) safe and what will risk that safety.

The need to cope with change

Change can be exciting, it can also increase fear and insecurity. Whereas settling into school for the first time, or into a new class, presents few problems to most children who adjust easily to new demands and expectations, for others change may be distressing. Some major events at home, including the birth of a new baby or changes in family structure may increase insecurity and affect behaviour. It is helpful for teachers to have at least some basic information about such matters as it helps them to understand what is going on for the child. Poor behaviour may, in fact, be more apparent at school because the child will not want to risk security further at home and may be keeping a low profile.

Children cope better with change when:

☛ They are given good information at an appropriate level about what to expect and/or what is happening.
☛ They are able to familiarise themselves with changes without too much happening all at once.
☛ They are given time to adapt to imminent changes.
☛ They can have a transitional object if needed.
☛ They are reassured as to the stability of other things.

☛ They are encouraged to anticipate new experiences positively as something fresh and exciting.

The need for love, affection and belonging

One teacher summed this up very effectively as she watched a young boy arrive into her class for the first time, pushing, shoving, shouting and looking miserably angry: 'That one's going to need a lot of loving!' This wasn't a sentimental statement, it was her way of trying to address the issues in terms of the child's needs in order that she would be able to fulfil her role as a teacher; it was an acknowledgement that in order to prevent difficulties from escalating she would have to be pro-active. This section looks more closely at what that statement might mean in everyday classroom management.

The need to be accepted

More than anything else all children, especially those who have a history of difficult behaviour, should feel that they are wanted in school and that they are seen as valuable and important. This is not easy for teachers who will be very concerned about meeting the needs of all their pupils and worry that those children who put extra demands on their time will make their job more stressful. Nevertheless the warmth, security and consistency that is available from caring teachers can be the difference that a child needs to make progress even though it may take some time for that development to manifest itself. Teachers often underestimate the great difference their approach makes to children's feelings of self-worth and consequently their behaviour.

In one school Christa was seen as 'a real pickle', an energetic ball of self-will who threw herself into everything – including tantrums. The teacher talked about her with a rueful smile on her face: 'She really wears me out sometimes but we just let her get on with it and sooner or later she realises that she'd rather be joining in with the rest of the group. Every time she starts we say "Here she goes again", but when it's over and done with she is reassured that we haven't rejected her because of her outburst. It's happening less and less. We all love her and I think she now knows it. It's taken an age but I think we're now round the corner.'

In another school Stephen was seen as a disruptive, disobedient young 'thug', a boy who went round the class interfering with other children's work and rarely doing anything constructive himself. The teacher was unable to find anything positive to say about him: 'He's just not a loveable child, he makes my life a misery, not to mention those of the other children. He hasn't got any friends at all – they all avoid him like the plague. I can't tell you how much attention he's taken up in the last week alone.' This child's experience of rejection continued until he was excluded from school.

Teachers need to separate out very clearly for children their acceptance of them and their rejection of their poor behaviour. Small children cannot but help take things personally so they will feel that if a teacher is cross or doesn't like what they do, then the teacher doesn't like them. Teachers can make it really clear what is unacceptable but also give positive messages to the child about herself.

61

LIVERPOOL HOPE UNIVERSITY

Showing acceptance

One way of showing acceptance to a child is to show interest. Infant teachers do this very effectively, asking children about holidays, new brothers and sisters and the welfare of pets. Listening to what they have to say is equally valuable. For children who may find themselves having more difficult conversations with teachers about behaviour it is especially important that opportunities are seized to find out and talk about other things to redress the balance. A quick word in passing is all that is needed to show a child that a teacher cares enough to remember what is important to them. Simply commenting on what a child is doing is also useful in many ways. Not only does it give messages of interest but it also provides the language to develop conceptual understanding, e.g. 'That's a wonderful train you are making with the Lego, haven't you put a lot of wheels on, can you help me count how many?'

Smiling is powerful. Across the world, across cultures, smiling is the universal sign of welcome. A direct and genuine smile to a child gives messages of warmth, of liking and of acceptance. When accompanied by good eye contact it can also be a great attention giver and reinforcer. If a child becomes used to such attention for behaving well the removal of positive expressions in 'ignoring' bad behaviour can also be very effective. Most teachers are naturally affectionate with small children. Concerns over abuse in recent years have made this more difficult. Many children do, however, seek out physical affection and withholding this could be seen as rejecting. A quick hug, a hand on the arm, a ruffled head are all warm messages of acceptance. If a child shies away from any of this then it is better to take the lead from the child. They may be very shy or physical contact has other connotations for them.

Teachers who set out to develop positive relationships with children in this way are more likely to have success with a range of other strategies which depend on the responses of someone 'significant' in the child's life. For these purposes a teacher becomes significant when the child cares about how they react, is more prepared to refer to them as a model and to listen to what they say because in the past this has included messages that have been 'easy to hear'.

The need to belong

As well as being accepted by their teachers, children need to feel that they belong to and are part of the class. Feeling that they are on the periphery and not having the confidence to be part of the group can distract children from learning. Chapter 9, 'Cooperation and the Group', looks more closely at the need to belong and discusses ways of welcoming children into school and developing a school and class identity. Children who are helped to feel that they belong have more to lose when their behaviour causes distress to their classmates.

The need to have friendly interactions with other children

Children can belong to many different groups; a family, a school, a class or a smaller friendship group. Having a friendship network becomes increasingly important as children get older but it is important that the initial learning for interactive skills is laid down at a younger age. Where good social behaviour has been modelled by adults and where there has been guidance in respect of basic collaborative skills then children will usually be able to quickly establish positive interactions in the classroom. Not all children, however, have had that experience or know what to do in a group and these pupils will need guidance and on occasions more direct teaching.

Figure 7.2 Belonging to a group

If children know what is friendly behaviour, and are given opportunities and encouragement to be friendly then this opens up the possibility of establishing friendships in the classroom. Where these alliances regularly raise the self-esteem of the children concerned, they can be powerful reinforcers for supporting learning and positive behaviours.

The need for self-esteem

Everyone needs to feel good about themselves, to have their strengths acknowledged and receive positive attention from others. Promoting the self-esteem of young children should be fully integrated into any learning programme, whether this is to develop conceptual and cognitive skills or to establish appropriate behaviours. A focus on the positive, commenting and praising the child for what she has managed to achieve rather than what she has failed to do, is the most effective way of maintaining both self-esteem and motivation. Where children are given things to do in which they can be successful, where mistakes are part of the learning process and where there is encouragement rather than condemnation then self-esteem is more likely to remain high. Teachers need to avoid statements which are tacked onto praise such as 'Why can't you always be like this?' as they refocus on the child's failures and inabilities.

Children who arrive in school with very negative feelings about themselves my require a specific programme to develop a more positive self-perception, such as making an 'I can' book. Other ideas for raising self-esteem can be found in other chapters.

The need to know how to express feelings.

Children may have limited understanding of their own feelings and restricted ways of expressing these. Talking about and acknowledging emotions, especially young children's own emotions, is not common practice within British society. You may, however, frequently hear adults comment about their own feelings to their children and these are often negative e.g. 'You make me so cross', 'You are driving me to distraction', 'I'm sick and tired of you doing that'. Much of this is not likely to help children develop either good self-esteem or an understanding of their own feelings, except possibly blame and guilt. Encouraging children to believe that they can engender good feelings in others by commenting on the positive is not only empowering but raises self-esteem and extends access to strategies for both emotional expression and management e.g.

☞ 'Your smiley face this morning makes me feel really cheerful too'.
'I'm so excited that you were able to read all those words today, aren't you?'
'Well, I guess we must both be happy that you have had a whole playtime playing nicely with your friends'.

Helping children to identify good feelings about themselves raises their self-esteem. They may then be more able to look at and articulate less positive feelings such as anger. In turn this promotes strategies for self-expression which isn't reliant on impulse and also helps to begin to link feelings with thoughts and actions.

The need for self-actualisation

This can be defined as the ability to reach our potential, to feel that we can be successful and have control over our destiny. Although young children are not at the stage of being able to conceptualise this in any real way the adults who are involved with them are often very conscious of aiming for this goal. In order for it to be reached there are several subsidiary needs.

Access to play and other learning opportunities

Children don't necessarily need a wide range of bought toys though these can, of course, be helpful. What they need is space to play, things they can use as play materials, guidance to extend their play skills, opportunities to engage in play with others and someone who will mediate their experiences, talk to them and help them make sense of their experiences. Lack of these opportunities in pre-school years can lead to difficulties when children are presented with what must appear to be a cornucopia of possibilities in the classroom. They will need guidance and limitations to focus and engage appropriately with what is on offer. Once they can do this they need to be allowed some freedom to be experimental and creative.

The need to be engaged in the learning process

Children whose more basic needs are not being met will find it much harder to be engaged with learning in any real way. Teachers often find that teaching does not necessarily mean that something has been learnt. Either the initial focus has not been sufficient and/or other factors have inhibited retention. Engaging a child on an affective level, both in terms of a high interest factor and feelings of success is therefore the first step to learning.

This includes helping him to relate and build new knowledge into existing structures.

The need to feel successful

For each individual person, success may mean something different. Success is defined not only by personal aspirations but by societal, cultural and institutional goals. It can be an very invidious concept, especially when judged competitively. For many people in the Western world success means having lots of material things or at least the wherewithal to own property. It also means high academic qualifications. Success as defined by other values such as personal qualities may be dismissed as not so important, although in effect they may be crucial to a person's success in being happy and fulfilled.

Figure 7.3 Certificates to acknowledge success in many areas

Success in all definitions, however, breeds success. Those individuals who feel they can be effective in their world, that they can achieve and feel good about themselves are those who are motivated to continue to aim high. They have usually set themselves realistic goals and have seen sufficient progress towards them to keep going. The same is true of children: they need to be presented with achievable targets, know that they can be successful in meeting them and also know that this pleases those who matter to them.

The need to develop an internal locus of control

People who have an external locus of control cannot develop self actualisation because they do not attribute either their successes or their failures to themselves. In their view, successes are due to luck and failures to other people, circumstances or fate. Secondary age pupils who find themselves in trouble for their behaviour are often quick to attribute blame elsewhere and are sometimes unable to see that there is anything within their own power which would have changed a situation. Children can be helped to develop an internal locus of control and feel that they can be effective by being offered choices. When it comes to behaviour in class a choice of consequences can be offered. This is effective both as a management strategy and to promote empowerment for the child. If you do *this* then you will be choosing *that*, e.g. 'If you choose to hide under the table during story you are choosing to stay in during playtime – if you choose to sit with us then you will be able to go out to play with everyone else'. The child can then be praised for making a good choice or have it pointed out to them that the consequence of staying in was their choice. The fact they don't like it may influence the choice they make next time.

Summary

All children have needs, for basic survival, for emotional and physical safety, to be loved and cared for, to feel good about themselves and to grow and develop at an optimum level. Some children have difficulties coping with the demands of school because their basic needs are not being met elsewhere. If there isn't an attempt to redress the balance in some way then efforts in delivering the curriculum may be limited. This doesn't mean that teachers have to take over the parenting role but they do need to be aware that some children have these needs, and that these needs may change in accordance with the changes in children's lives. It is probably most effective in terms of time and resources to incorporate strategies to meet these needs into the daily life of the classroom.

CHAPTER 8

FEELING COMFORTABLE, FEELING CONFIDENT

As anyone who has ever started a new job will know, it can take considerable time to 'settle in' and become a productive worker: time to find out what happens in a particular institution, who to approach for help/support/everyday items, and who has responsibility for what. The same is true for children starting at school. One of the main functions of school is to create an environment in which learning can take place. Unless children feel comfortable and confident in their school environment, then this fundamental objective is less likely to be achieved. This is likely to involve a high initial investment of time and energy, but will pay excellent dividends later for all concerned. This chapter clarifies what children need to know in their first days and weeks which will make them feel more at ease. We look at ways in which this can be taught so that there is little room for doubt as to what happens and what is expected.

Getting to know who is who and what is where

The move into reception is a big change for all children, but more so if they have not had access to formal pre-school experiences.

Whatever the situation, school will be different from home and some pupils will take longer to settle than others. Some children will be anxious and do nothing until they are told, whilst others will simply do as they like, until told differently. Young children will be more likely to comply with requests and to behave better, when they know what to do and expectations are made clear.

The process of familiarising young children with the school environment needs to include:

- the names and roles of adults with whom they come into regular contact
- the layout of the classroom and the location of everyday items within it
- the layout of the school
- the structure of the school day
- the way things are done – common routines
- school and classroom rules.

Adults in the school context

If parents and pupils have made visits prior to starting in reception class they may have met their teacher-to-be, possibly their classroom assistant if there is one and they may have seen other adults in passing. There are, however, a number of other adults with whom they will regularly come into contact. These include the other teachers, school secretary, midday supervisors, welfare person, classroom assistants, caretaker, and any other adults who work in the school on a regular basis.

Parents as well as pupils need the opportunity to familiarise themselves with these people, and their roles and responsibilities.

☛ One way that many schools do this is to have labelled photographs of all staff on a notice board in the main entrance to the school, with their names and titles. These photographs need to be positioned so that they are accessible to small children, and need to be regularly updated with any staffing changes. The issue of pupils' safety at school has become increasingly important and parents want to be reassured about who has access to, and who will be responsible for the care of, their children during the school day.

☛ Another useful way to familiarise pupils with the adults around them is by the use of simple jigsaws made from photographs of those adults. These can be obtained relatively cheaply from photographic outlets, but some schools have made simpler ones themselves, or with the help of a parent.

☛ It is also possible to use smaller photographs mounted on card and laminated, to construct simple matching games for pupils to use.

☛ When they are familiar with some names, children can be taken in small groups to various parts of the school to find out where different people are usually located. This has an added advantage in helping pupils orient their classroom within the school as a whole and facilitates a greater understanding of the roles of other adults.

☛ Photographs of the adults can be placed on the door of the room in which they are located.

☛ Later on, when the class has become established, a class photograph can be displayed on the classroom door.

Often overlooked is the important role that the dinner supervisors can have in the life of very young pupils. It would seem beneficial that the same supervisor is allocated to a class for a given period of time so that relationships can be established. Sometimes this is not possible and there has to be rotation or sharing of staff. Whatever is the norm in a particular school, it is important that introductions take place formally: 'This is Miss .... if you are hurt or need help, she will be in the playground today so you can go to her.'

☛ In one school, everyone, staff and pupils alike, wears a name badge for the first few weeks. This helps everyone get to know each other on a more individual basis. The use of children's names by all staff supports a welcoming ethos.

It is important to remember that, as with other learning, this process of familiarisation has to be done more than once, and it does no harm to repeat various aspects of it every so often. If there is a new child in the class, or a new adult arrives, this gives pupils the opportunity to demonstrate their knowledge of who is who and enhances a sense of independence and responsibility.

Figure 8.1 Our Dinner Lady

The layout of the classroom

Familiarity and routine are central to the development of confidence and security. This needs to be established within the classroom prior to extension beyond it.

In order to increase independence in learning, children need to be able to find what they need for each activity and return equipment to its proper place after use.

☛ This can be made significantly easier if there are containers with drawings or photographs on the outside which indicate their use. Words may be used as well, but consideration needs to be given to non-readers, and to pupils whose first language is not English. Sometimes a colour code can be used if objects are stored according to colour alone. Tidying away then becomes a maths activity of sorting and matching.

☛ Silhouettes or outlines of objects, can be drawn to mark their location on the wall, inside the cupboard door, etc.

Figure 8.2 Silhouettes and labels

- Once children understand that there is a place for everything, then 'finished' and 'unfinished' work trays can be included. Some children may have problems with the concept of 'finished' and this will need to be made explicit.
- A fun way to practice locating objects as a class, is to have a collection of everyday objects on a tray/in a box, and with the teacher removing one at a time, and asking for volunteers to demonstrate by putting it away, where it belongs, to the rest of the class.
- Similarly, when gathered on the carpet, pupils can be asked to point to – 'the book corner/where we put the lunch boxes/where we keep the Lego' etc., with everyone pointing as appropriate.
- Signs with words and symbols can indicate how many children can use an area at one time (3 stick people drawn to indicate 3 children) e.g. at the sand tray.

Figure 8.3 Learning where things are kept

Elsewhere in the school

Children will need to establish the whereabouts of other locations. These could include the toilets, the cloakroom, and where to go for a late mark if they arrive after the register has been taken. Although it is time consuming, if an adult accompanies the children to various places for the first few weeks, it will pay dividends later.

The playground

Playtimes can be a stressful time for many children and especially so for the child just starting school. It may be the first time that they have been in the playground with older pupils and no doubt it appears to be a vast place by comparison to the smaller, more secure areas they have been used to.

- In some schools the playground is divided up into discrete areas of use, but the divisions may not be physically apparent. Plastic cones, used tyres, painted markings on the ground and the use of natural features such as hedges can help.

☞ Similarly, an adult can explore each area with a group of children, asking: 'Are we allowed to play football in this area?', 'Is this an area where it is safe to run?', with the children being expected to answer each question in each location.

Children in nursery schools may have been used to having outdoor toys such as bikes and scooters to play with and they may not know how to usefully use their time when these are not available.

☞ Teaching simple games in PE that can be used by children in the playground can be very helpful. An adult has merely to start off the game at playtime and then leave it to continue its course. It is particularly valuable if parent visitors, especially from other cultures, can be involved in the teaching of games to pupils throughout the school.

☞ Some schools have capitalised on the time and talent of parents, using their help to paint markings on the asphalt in the playground, for pupils to use to play games. These include Hopscotch, coloured circles, number snakes, and so on. There is no reason why walls could not be similarly utilised.

Figure 8.4 Games to play outdoors and indoors

Schools have tackled reception class playtimes in different ways:

● reception and nursery children having playtimes together
● reception children having playtime in the larger playground, at a different time from the rest of the school
● reception children having separate playtimes at the beginning, and sharing with older pupils after one or two terms.

☞ Those schools which foster a sense of caring and responsibility encourage older pupils to 'look after' or 'buddy' younger ones. This has to be presented as a high-status role and be rewarded at appropriate times by being drawn to everyone's attention as an act of kindness. It is surprising how significant this initiative can be in making playtimes happier for all concerned, and the ramifications it has across the whole school.

The school day – when things happen

The concept of time, the sequence of and connections between the events in the school day will be of differing significance for different children.

The intake of any reception class will include children whose home life is structured and organised so that various activities take place at set times in the day or week, and others who experience much less structure, where events might be much less predictable, and appear unconnected. It is important for the security of children that they have a general understanding of the structure, routines and timings of the school day. Most will not have a significant awareness of time passing, or be able to tell the time, but they need to have an idea of the meaning of: 'a few minutes', 'in a little while', 'after play', 'after lunch', and 'at home time'. They will also need an understanding, for example, that playtime comes after assembly, that library time is after lunch, and that home time comes after the story on the carpet, and so on.

The following ideas have all been used:

☛ The emphasis that one activity follows another, e.g. reminding pupils that after play, there will be the sharing of fruit. This can then have a third activity added on, so that a longer sequence is remembered.

☛ The making of a frieze with pupils, extending along a long wall outside, or within the classroom, depicting the various activities of the school day. A clock face could be included with each frame. Children's drawings or photographs of the children in each activity could be used. A backing sheet with pictures depicting the activities of the school day, could be placed behind the clock on the wall. The explicit use of vocabulary (before, next, after) may be necessary for some pupils, and encouragement of carers to use these words with children when they look at the frieze with them.

☛ Schedules using stick figures and symbols or photographs to represent various activities, with a moveable pointer, such as an arrow, to indicate to children what they will be doing next. Colour coding each activity may help further.

Figure 8.5 The sequence of a day

☛ Commercially produced picture cards are valuable for learning about and practising the sequences of many everyday activities.

Learning how things happen in and around school

Children might learn very quickly that after a short while in the classroom on a Monday morning, they will go into the hall for assembly. They soon come to learn that playtime is followed by the sharing of fruit and to associate the washing of hands with lunch time. This is *what* happens. The *how* is more difficult to establish! Teachers may expect that the children will walk quietly, not run, or push and shove, etc., but the expectations that teachers have of behaviour in school may be very different to those experienced elsewhere.

Teachers have sound reasons for the requests made to children, either health and safety, or the progress of their academic or social learning. At times, however, the reasons are not apparent or children may not have the necessary language, understanding or experience to comply. It is also not appropriate for teachers to have to justify all of their requests to pupils.

Rules

There may be several different types of rules in operation within a school. Classroom rules sometimes vary slightly from school rules. There may be rules specifically to deal with Health and Safety issues, rules about playtime, and rules for Circle work. (See Chapter 9, 'Cooperation and the Group').

What is important is that rules are few, and clearly and positively stated. If rules state 'do' rather than 'don't', it may be easier for children to remember them. Many young children hear the word 'don't' too often. Examples of rules are:

- Speak in a quiet voice in the classroom.
- Put up your hand if you want help.

Long lists of prohibited actions and the use of vague concepts such as *respect* are not helpful.

Some teachers of older classes may involve their pupils in the formulation of rules, on the premise that they will be more likely to keep to the rules if they have had some part in the decision making process. It is unlikely that many teachers of Infant classes would attempt to involve the pupils in this process at the start of the year.

Other teachers decide on the rules for their own classroom without involving pupils.

Both can be effective if the teachers are comfortable, the rules are few, simple, positively expressed and consistently applied.

Teaching a procedure/routine to young children

When teaching a new procedure/routine for the first time, it is often necessary to break it up into a number of simpler steps and teach them one at a time first. The children will then practice smaller routines separately, before amalgamating them together. Each of these smaller routines must, however, have a meaning for the child. An example of this would be when children are taught to tidy up the carpet area after choosing time. They would be taught to put the equipment into its container as a first step, be able to do that in a number of settings, then learn to put the containers on the correct shelf, and finally, in the correct cupboard. For more complex routines this might take a little time, but it will save a lot of time and effort later. A useful way of thinking of this is to compare the method to the way in which we might teach a child to dress or undress themselves – a series of small steps that complete a sequence.

For many children, an explanation alone is not sufficient. It is always important to demonstrate as well as explain what is expected, particularly for those who have language, hearing or attention problems. With younger children in particular, it is particularly important where possible to engage all their senses.

Children can then copy and practice what is expected. Individuals who are happy to do so, can be asked to demonstrate to the rest of the class. At this point, the class can be asked to give positive feedback, and constructive criticism: e.g. 'That was very good, ... has sat down with his arms folded. How could we *all* do this better next time?'

It is important to remember, as the term goes on, that there may be a need to go back to practising some routines from time to time.

N.B. If any child persists in non-compliance, then it is worth checking their level of comprehension of the task as a first step. (See Chapter 11, 'The Hard To Manage Child')

Movement around the school

Once expectations are clear, then movement around the school can be taught as any other routine. What is different is that the whole class may not be visible all at the same time. Issues of Health and Safety are important to remember, particularly for example on stairs.

The following ideas have been helpful in managing movement around the school:

- ☛ 'I can' (walk sensibly down the corridor) badges for a few children at a time.
- ☛ Signs suspended from the ceiling: 'Thank you for walking nicely.' It is worth remembering that these will need to be read out, and commented on by the teacher.
- ☛ One school teaches children to ensure that they don't walk any closer than an arm's length behind the pupil in front. This prevents congestion in doorways, and pushing and shoving.
- ☛ Where there are two adults in a class, the children can be lined up at one doorway, and be sent off by one adult, a few at a time, to another end of the corridor, where they are met by the second adult. Another group will be sent when the previous one has arrived and is settled/quiet. This teaches children to move about in an orderly fashion, and can equally be applied to moving about in other situations, e.g. from tables to the carpet – one group has to be settled before another joins them.
- ☛ Transitions between activities can be more successful if the children arrive at the second activity when there is already something exciting happening, rather than having to wait perhaps for a teacher, or other members of the class to arrive. This isn't always possible, however.

- If there are separate entrances for Infant and Junior classes, then this can be indicated by marking each route with small and larger footprints painted on the ground. Further distinction can be obtained by using two different colours of paint.
- Many schools have put brightly coloured arrows on corridors and stairs to show children which side to walk.
- A red line painted at eye level on the wall, can indicate the way to the school office.

Giving notice and gaining children's attention

Young children get so involved in activities that they may need a warning that it is about to stop. After all, many adults are reluctant to abandon those activities that they are enjoying. There needs to be sufficient warning: a few seconds is not enough.

- A simple: 'We are going to tidy up in a few minutes' may be sufficient for the majority, whereas others may need the direction preceded by their name. It is important that this is done quietly, or from close by, to avoid negative labelling.
- It is possible to give a warning with a bell, for example that signals two more minutes to the end of playtime.
- One teacher rings a bell or triangle when the noise level gets too much. Another teacher hums gently at this point, and the class quietens.
- Rather than shout to get the attention in a busy class, it is possible to teach them that when they see a simple non-verbal signal e.g. the teacher with a finger on her lip, hand in the air, or on the head, that they must look at her, copy her, and remain silent. Gradually, the noise level drops, and a new instruction can be given to the class.

Figure 8.6 'Show me you're listening'

Summary

Settling into a new environment can be a stressful experience for anyone. Young children are no exception to this. They will settle more quickly, because they will have a greater understanding of what it means to behave, and be ready to embark on more formal learning, if they are explicitly taught how to do what is expected of them (both in the classroom and outside it). If children are prepared for the changes that occur throughout the school day, and in the life of the school, this will increase their sense of security. Children who feel comfortable and confident in the school environment are likely to experience academic and social success which is what teachers want for their pupils.

MAKING EXPECTATIONS EXPLICIT

Make requests clear and succinct – use visual cues as well as words.

Model to the pupils what they are expected to do.

Keep it simple – break down tasks to simple steps and teach each step separately before amalgamating them.

Have an expectation of compliance and ensure this is explicit.

Give reminders before reprimands.

Pay particular attention to the beginnings and ends of activities.

TEACHING A ROUTINE TO YOUNG CHILDREN

For lining up, sitting on the carpet, walking along a corridor, getting ready for PE etc:

Gain the children's attention and ensure that those with the most difficulty listening are closest to the teacher.

Explain carefully and simply what you want the children to do.

Tell them how you expect them to do it.

Demonstrate to the children what you have asked them to do.

Get the children to practice what it is you want them to learn.

Discuss with the children what they have practised, using praise as appropriate.

Remind the children of expectations each time they carry out a routine, until they can do it without prompting.

Withdraw prompts gradually but continue to comment positively on achievement.

Use the children's knowledge and skills to help a new entrant to the class to learn your expectations.

CHAPTER 9

COOPERATION AND THE GROUP

In this section, consideration is given to the factors that determine how successful young children will be as members of a group. The skills that teachers need to teach in order to make this possible and activities and ideas that may facilitate this are discussed. This includes some ideas for developing Circle Work with young children.

Fitting in and feeling special

Although young children find it quite difficult to share naturally, we expect them to share both toys and materials in the infant classroom as well as the time and attention of the adults around. Some children need to learn this skill from scratch as they will have had little opportunity to do so in their early years.

Not all adults are able to cooperate with one another all of the time and it is important that we do not expect children to consistently reach standards of behaviour that we do not always manage ourselves.

Teachers use the word cooperation to express two different aspects of children's behaviour. They may refer to a child who does as they are told as being 'cooperative', or they may talk generally about children who can learn and play cooperatively with each other. This chapter is about cooperation and the group.

What is cooperation?

Cooperation is an intrinsic part of the human condition, exemplified by centuries of achievement. In some societies it is only the cooperative endeavour that ensures survival.

Cooperation involves active participation in a group, membership of which may be lifelong, e.g. family and some religious groups, or of shorter duration, e.g. a sports club, play group. In the infant classroom duration of group membership may range from very brief, perhaps a matter of minutes for some activities and games, to much longer in the case of class and year groupings.

Being a successful member of any group requires the ability to relate positively to members of that group, although not necessarily with all members at all times, and being able to work together in the interests of everyone. Although different pupils bring different skills to the task, positive relationships within any group depend upon:

- sufficient confidence to be an active member but sufficient social awareness and skills not to dominate
- socially acceptable behaviour, as determined by formal and unwritten rules
- the ability to listen, to communicate verbally and non-verbally, and to express feelings appropriately.

What is involved in cooperation?

Cooperation is most clearly demonstrated by those who are able to share and turn-take in various activities, in other words are capable of 'give and take'.

In order to cooperate with a group, children need to:

- learn to feel positive about themselves
- learn to feel positive about being part of the group
- acquire the necessary cooperative skills
- be able to use the skills appropriately.

Children learning to feel positive about themselves

The importance of self-esteem

There is much evidence to indicate strong links between good self-esteem and academic and social success. Before children can develop a concern for the feelings and perspectives of others, they must attend to their own emotional needs, and feel good about themselves. Only then will they be able to work and play collaboratively and cooperatively with others.

Indicators and outcomes of high self-esteem

When children have experienced encouragement and praise and have had opportunities for social and personal success they are more likely to perceive themselves as capable, likeable and worthwhile. When people feel positive about themselves and have high self-esteem, then they:

- are able to feel secure in their abilities
- are less afraid of making mistakes and more able to learn from the ones that they do make
- are more willing to try something different or difficult
- are more able to learn from criticism
- can view failures in a balanced and realistic way
- are more trusting
- can be outgoing, and positive towards others in words and actions
- do not have to 'fight their own corner' with peers
- are more likely to establish rewarding friendships.

Indicators and outcomes of low self-esteem

- Children with low self-esteem and a low opinion of their abilities may be unable to accept praise because they feel it is not sincere. This may be because it doesn't fit in with their own views, or they believe that the person who praises them has an ulterior motive.

79

LIVERPOOL HOPE UNIVERSITY COLLEGE

- They are often isolated at playtime or in class. Some do not seek to join in for fear of being rejected, or because they believe that no one likes them. Sometimes quite innocuous comments and actions are perceived in the wrong way or taken personally e.g. a child with low self-esteem bumped accidentally by the child sitting next to him may find it hard to accept that it was an accident, believing that it was deliberate – an attack on their person.
- Children develop an external locus of control – i.e. everything is someone else's fault, because blaming others for what happens seems less damaging to their self-esteem.
- The same child may find it difficult to accept that a reprimand simply means that the teacher is unhappy with something they have done, feeling instead that the teacher does not like them.
- They may underachieve academically if fear of failure or ridicule prevents them from tackling new work. Some children develop a repertoire of work avoidance strategies – much to the frustration of their teachers.
- A child will sometimes cover feelings of inferiority by becoming the class clown or by daring to do things that shock in an effort to gain status with their peers. Acting as the class clown may also be done to divert attention away from the difficulties that an individual is facing with the work.
- They may set high unrealistic standards for themselves, and become frustrated at any mistake they make – hence the constant rubbing out. This is sometimes accompanied by the destruction of their own work and that of others as they make unfavourable comparisons.
- Unrealistic parental expectations can exacerbate low self-esteem.
- Some children are very anxious, and need constant reassurance.
- Some are very disruptive, either as one way of guaranteeing attention, or as a result of frustration.

In short, those with low self esteem may exhibit defensive, hostile, destructive or withdrawn behaviour.

Within any classroom there are some individuals who are unable to share toys, equipment, adult time and attention etc with peers, and are consequently involved in frequent squabbles. They may become marginalised, either because they do not have the necessary skills for play or because they try to dominate. Teachers have to encourage other pupils to accept these individuals as they lack friendship skills of their own and are not ready with kind deeds or words for others.

Enhancing the self-esteem of young children – helping children to feel positive about themselves

Infant teachers are usually very sensitive to the self-esteem needs of small children when they first start school. It may be later on when a child begins to realise that she is not learning to read as quickly as her classmates or when emotions are out of control that more concerted efforts need to be made to maintain a vulnerable self-esteem.

The following are some of the many strategies that teachers have used to enhance self-esteem:

☞ Remembering the personal details of children and their families, making an effort to ask things of individual children, noticing small changes and positively commenting on them.

☞ Developing positive gender and racial attitudes, and celebrating diversity within the class and the community. This could include visits and talks by various members of the wider community, as well as the use of appropriate posters and books. It is important that racist and other name-calling be dealt with quickly.

☞ Avoiding making self fulfilling prophecies where a false expectation of failure/poor behaviour results in exactly that e.g. 'This class is the noisiest one I've come across.' Here, the class will come to believe just that, and there will be no motivation for the class to be anything else.

☞ Avoiding making value judgements based on family, culture, ethnicity or gender which can be very damaging. This is particularly true in the case of assumptions about the academic achievement of children whose first language is not English, and children from socially and economically disadvantaged families.

☞ Keeping calm and using a quiet voice when issuing a reprimand. Some pupils associate shouting or raised voices with other situations and respond badly. If teachers limit the occasions when they use a loud voice, it will be all the more effective when they do. Children can become accustomed to a raised voice, and it becomes part of the background noise that they learn to ignore. In the words of one teacher: 'Use it wisely or wear it out.'

☞ Labelling the behaviour as undesirable, not the child.

☞ If it is necessary to reprimand a child, then looking for an opportunity to praise them for something as soon as possible afterwards.

☞ Trying to give every pupil specific praise once a day for something.

☞ Giving praise for being brave enough to try: too often the focus is on the product rather than the process of learning.

☞ Avoiding making comparisons between children (especially siblings).

☞ Instead of making such statements as: 'Who is the first to be ready?', which implies that there are those who will not be successful, saying: 'Who is sitting nicely?'

☞ Working with other school staff who have contact with the pupils, such as lunch time supervisors, to establish a shared sense of values and develop a statement on self-esteem within the school behaviour policy.

☞ Saying something positive about a child's achievements to someone else in their hearing can be more effective than direct praise.

A personal space/place and sense of self

Many young children will bring with them, when they first start school, a transition object from home: it may be a piece of blanket or a soft toy that they need for security. This will be abandoned when the child is ready. For some children, this needs to be a gradual process whereby the object is left on the teacher's desk/shelf, and later on, in the child's bag until the end of the day. The next step is when the parent takes the object home and brings it back to greet the child at the end of the day. At the end of this process the object should be left at home, but getting to this stage will take longer for some children than others.

Children need to be helped to maintain a sense of self in the new, larger, school environment. It can be hard for some to be part of a larger group and yet maintain a sense of self.

The following ideas have been used:

☞ Name badges for all new children, for the first few weeks.
☞ Many schools will use a photograph/favourite picture and text to indicate where an individual child hangs their coat, or which drawer is their own.
☞ A shelf/drawer similarly labelled, on which to put a packed lunch/personal possession/construction. This reinforces the concepts of 'yours' and 'mine'.
☞ A personalised cup, if it is the practice to have something to drink after play.
☞ Pupils are asked to paint a self-portrait. (They may benefit from using mirrors to observe themselves first.) This can be repeated each term. One teacher has placed successive self portraits on top of each other, and the children have the opportunity to discover how they have changed, and also how their skills improve.

Learning to belong

Feeling positive about the group

A sense of belonging and being part of a group is very powerful and can help children to have a positive identity and raise their self-esteem. To feel positive about membership of a group, children need to feel that being in that group is rewarding to them. Circle time activities described later are very valuable for this. The following may also help children to identify with the group and feel a commitment to it:

☞ On the outside of the classroom door, putting up a 'Welcome to (...............) class.' sign, with small self-portraits of all of the children in the class mounted on card.
☞ One school has repeat photo sessions halfway through the first term, with a theme of 'This is our class at work'. This reinforces pupils' expectations and is an excellent way of communicating with parents about what is happening in school for their child.
☞ Making simple, positive statements about the class and displaying these statements prominently, e.g. suspended from the ceiling. Any visitor can then read them out. Such statements might include:
  • 'Yellow class works quietly.'
  • 'Class 2 help each other.'
  • 'Blue class welcomes (the name of a new child).'
  • 'Class 1 did a great assembly'.
☞ Setting up areas within the classroom which are the responsibility of pairs or groups of pupils e.g. watering the plants, sharpening the pencils, or tidying the book corner at the end of the day. This must be presented as a high status job, and not a chore, and one in which the group endeavour is important.
☞ Developing larger whole class pieces of work, e.g. a class mural or frieze, involving all children in the planning of class assemblies. This encourages group ownership as well as group membership. Displays outside the classroom are even more effective as they promote

recognition of class efforts from the wider school community.

☛ Making sure that there are opportunities for public praise for whole class achievements.

☛ Discussions about how to keep in contact with classmates who may be away for a long time because they are ill – sending regular pictures and taped or written messages – this communicates that all class members are important and that the whole group have a responsibility towards each other.

☛ Several teachers have a teddy which they move around from table to table during working sessions: 'Teddy likes to sit with those groups who are working well together.'

☛ A similar ploy is to put a marble in a jar every time a group works well – when the jar is full the whole class have a treat. This could be used as a whole class jar, or a jar for each table. When a child who has difficulties is given a marble for his good behaviour and this benefits the whole group it enhances his acceptance and increases peer support.

☛ Although rewards for appropriate behaviours are a positive way of encouraging cooperation it is also valuable to offer treats to the class that are unconditional and are intended to develop a class identity by sharing an experience.

☛ It is useful to have some system whereby the children signal their presence in school. This can be done when a name tag with Velcro or one with a loop is placed on an illustrated board by each child as they enter the classroom. This can serve a number of functions: it can be a matching activity, it encourages independence, and it establishes a routine at the start of the day, as well as engendering a sense of belonging to a defined group.

Figure 9.1 Displaying statements about the class

The importance of humour

Most young children have a well developed sense of humour – though not a very subtle one! Five year old children are often highly amused by playing with words, sharing jokes and the similarities and differences between people. A good way of promoting a class identity is for the class to share laughter. A funny story, or a poem, can provide an enjoyable shared moment. The frequent use of the words 'we' and 'us' emphasises the inclusion of everyone in such experiences: 'Well, we did all enjoy that didn't we?' However, it is important to be clear that we are laughing with, rather than laughing at someone, the latter being damaging to self-esteem.

Teachers also need to be aware that children who are not confident with language or who are in the early stages of English acquisition may feel excluded from some aspects of humour and providing a visual component where possible may enable them genuinely to share in the laughter.

Making sure no-one is left out

It is important to be aware of potential negative effects of strong groups, and to ensure that no-one is excluded. Encouraging different groupings and partnerships is important. There are many ways in which this can be done.

☞ Children are asked to go out into the playground, line up form teams etc according to different groups, e.g.
  – all who are wearing..............
  – those with a name beginning with...........
  – those who came to school on foot/ by car/on the bus.

This also helps pupils to understand that they can belong to many groups and is a useful way to introduce and celebrate diversity.

Other children could be encouraged to help those who might be having difficulty knowing if they are in this group or not. This is especially true of children who are new to the English language – some visual support would also be helpful.

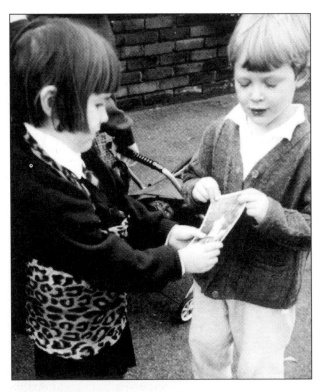

Figure 9.2 Matching the halves of a picture to find a partner

☞ Instead of 'choosing a partner', for instance in PE, old postcards/birthday cards can be cut in half and given out randomly. Children then work with the partner who has the matching card. This may need to be practised in a small group setting first. This extra visual support is useful for many children, especially those new to the English language.

Developing cooperative skills

The following includes some ways in which teachers have fostered awareness of the skills needed for cooperation.

Friendship skills

It is important for children to know what it means to be friendly and to learn the skills involved in positive interactions. The following have had a positive impact on the peer relationships in infant classes:

☞ Developing a friendship 'project' with the whole class – what are friendly things to do?
☞ As part of one friendship project a 'play stop' was placed in the playground and anyone who wanted to join in a game would go and stand there. Other children were expected to ask that child to play.
☞ Using stickers which say: 'I was a good friend today' – given for specific behaviours. Here it is important to keep a record of who has been in receipt, to ensure that no-one is left out.
☞ Preparing classroom notes which praise children for positive friendly behaviours. Put them on the child's table or chair after playtime, e.g. 'Thank you for making a space for Liam in the line before play', 'I saw you let Charlene be the baby in the home corner this morning when you really wanted to be the baby – well done'. It's a great motivator for reading – if they can't work it out themselves, the children will quickly ask someone what their note says.
☞ Making a friendship tree. Children are awarded a 'leaf' for friendly acts and this is placed on the tree – the tree therefore 'grows' with friendship.

Learning to play together

Some children come to school with little experience of collaborative play. Other children have had little access to play materials or play opportunities. Children of homeless or refugee families may be particularly disadvantaged in this respect.

☞ Some teachers have found it useful to carry out role-plays themselves, with children watching, e.g. in the home corner. The children not only find this reversal great fun, but it helps them develop their play skills. Supervised and supported play can also be helpful. This involves an adult making suggestions, giving a commentary or directing play interactions. This could happen either between two children or between an adult and child.

Teachers need to be aware that some children can be very dominant in play situations and ensure that all children are given opportunities to take the lead. Letting individual children lead class games from time to time means that they look for the same sort of cooperative behaviour from others as the teacher does. The following are examples of simple cooperative games which can be taught in PE lessons and then played in the playground.

Mirrors: With children in pairs, they face each other and try to do exactly the same movements at the same time.

Shadows: This is the same idea but with one child behind the other.

Simon/Sally says: One child is the leader and carries out a number of movements saying 'Simon (or Sally) says do this'. If they do not use the expression 'Simon says', then anyone doing the action is out. A variation on this would be to use the name of the person who is Star of the Day (see later).

Animals: A pack of cards is handed out to all the children. The cards are pictures of animals – there are four of each. No-one may look at their card until a given signal. The idea is that they meet up with others in their group by making the appropriate animal noises. (Care needs to be taken not to disturb other classes!) Teachers will need to check that children know what noises different animals make.

Figure 9.3 Playing 'mirrors'

Body letters: Children form letters by curling their bodies into the correct shapes. This could be done standing up or flat on the floor. A letter *b* would require one child as the upright and another as the round part. This is an activity that would supplement teaching done in class, and can be extended to promote phonic awareness.

As well as teaching games in class and PE that children can use at playtime, it is helpful if lunch time supervisory staff have a repertoire of games to teach/play with children.

Helping

Many primary aged children define a friend as 'Someone who helps you'. Therefore children need to learn concrete examples of what that means in practice. The following ideas support the development of these concepts:

- Ensuring that praise is given for any acts of caring, sharing, etc, so that pupils begin to feel that those acts are both noticed and valued.
- Within the classroom and school, identifying the role of 'helper' as very high status can be a reward in itself e.g. going on an errand for the Head teacher, or escorting a child to another room.
- Developing topic work on a theme of 'People who help us'. This can be within the school, or the wider community. It could include a board in the classroom with drawings of children in the class who have been helpful. These persons can be nominated by the class members themselves, and by adults who notice positive behaviour.
- Highlighting helpful actions publicly at the class 'Good News' time, at whole school assemblies, to parents/carers or to anyone who will listen!
- There is a gender bias in 'helping' skills and boys may need extra guidance and encouragement.

Figure 9.4 Helping

Caring

- Keeping a class pet to encourage caring skills. Class discussions about the animal's needs can be related to the needs of others.
- When a new child starts at school giving other children the responsibility for taking care of them e.g. at playtime. Their role and the extent of their responsibility needs to be clear so that it doesn't become a burden.

Being fair and being seen to be fair

Learning to take turns

All teachers are conscientious about trying to be fair to children in their class. Being part of a larger group requires young children to be able to accept that there will be many occasions when they will have to wait their turn. Knowing that everyone has a turn makes the world of a young child more predictable, and therefore safer. Many will need reassurance that they

Figure 9.5 Making sure no-one misses their turn

will get their chance, time for attention etc. and that the choice is not random, or due to favouritism. Some systems for making this explicit are:

☛ **The Rota Wheel.** Two large cardboard wheels are made, with a smaller one inside the larger. Around the outside wheel are the names of jobs/activities (or their symbols) and around the inner wheel, the names of children or groups. The inner wheel is rotated daily, so that each person/all groups have a turn.

☛ A list by the door or elsewhere in the classroom, with a sliding pointer, to indicate who is first in line, who takes the register etc. This provides a focus for those who are waiting their turn, in that they can see their name, and watch the pointer move closer towards it, over time.

☛ A book of turns. This is used for any activities such as cooking, visiting the library, that take place outside of the classroom. Whenever a group is selected, their names or the name of the group, go in a small book.

☛ A name can be drawn out of one container, to indicate whose turn it is. At the end of the day/the next day, that name is placed in a different container, and a new one chosen. (Careful choice of see-through containers can be useful for predicting how many are left.)

☛ **Star of the Day:** Children become the Star of the Day automatically when their name is the next on the list. It is not connected with being deserving and no-one gets left out for any reason. Children who are absent on their day get fitted in when they return. The star of the day has privileges which could include the following:
  ● wear a special badge
  ● be first in line
  ● take the register
  ● feed the pets
  ● do the special jobs
  ● choose the story

- give out the fruit
- have their name on the board
- be the centre of the circle in Circle Time (see later)

Fairness doesn't always mean everyone getting exactly the same. Fairness is dealing with individuals according to their needs. When a teacher has to give extra attention to needy individuals, then this can be explained sensitively to children, and then it will be accepted as normal, especially if it is made explicit that everyone needs extra help from time to time.

Figure 9.6 Star of the day

Communication skills

The majority of pupils entering primary schools will have sufficient communication skills to make their needs known. Membership of a group however, requires an awareness of others, and some children may need to develop their perceptual skills generally, as a precursor to this. The following activities have been found helpful.

Teach observation skills

☛ Play games such as **Kim's Game**. It is fun to play a version of this with children e.g. everyone looks very carefully at two children for one minute – they then go out of the room and remove or change something about their appearance, such as exchanging jumpers, socks, hair clips. The class have to discover what it is. When someone has discovered the change they fold their arms. At the end of one minute everyone calls out the change.

Work on listening skills

☛ Teach what is involved in good listening. This would include facing the person you are talking to, using eye contact etc. Ask children to demonstrate how they show that they are listening.
☛ One teacher goes through a chant accompanied with actions, with pupils: 'We listen with our ears (they touch their ears), look with our eyes, (they

Figure 9.7 Sticker for good listening

touch their eyes), think with our brain (they touch their forehead) and we sit with our hands together (they do this).'

☞ **Are you listening?** One good game to encourage listening skills is for the teacher to ask certain children to stand up and turn round every time a character or object in a story is mentioned. A more demanding version of this is for the teacher to ask children to give her the names of people or things and the teacher weaves a story around this. The children are more focused but there is no visual support for those with greater language difficulties, and this might be problematic for such children.

Raise awareness of body language and expressions

☞ Ask a child to look cross, happy, miserable, frightened or ask them to draw a picture of themselves at a time when they were happy/sad etc. This can be used as the basis for class discussion.

☞ Cut out magazine/newspaper photographs of faces with different expressions and use them to promote discussion within the class, about what those expressions might mean.

Teach how to show interest

☞ Children are encouraged to find out about each other, especially those things they have in common. This needs to be highly structured for young children who may need help in knowing which questions to ask. Even at this age they can be encouraged to ask open-ended questions rather than closed ones, e.g. 'Which television programmes do you watch?' rather than 'Do you watch Cartoon Time?' Telling the whole group about each other also helps attention and memory skills, self-esteem, confidence and friendship.

Modelling good communication skills

When communicating with children teachers have found that it is useful to be aware of the following:

☞ Trying not to interrupt when children are speaking or at least wait until they pause for breath.

☞ Having an awareness of what the child's own body language may be conveying.

90

Figure 9.8 Modelling good communication skills

☞ Being aware of what the teacher's body language may be conveying to the child. Some children will pay more attention to body language than to words. Other children may misinterpret body language, according to their early experiences.

☞ Non-verbal communication can be very effective: the use of 'thumbs-up' when a teacher is pleased with what a child has done, a finger on the lips to indicate that silence is required, or just 'the look' that says to the child: 'I can see what you are doing, and I'm not pleased'.

Developing situation specific skills

Apart from teaching social skills generally, there are some situations, which may happen more frequently, where it may be useful to teach specifically for those settings. This can be particularly beneficial for children with social communication or language difficulties. Some ways that teachers have done this are as follows:

☞ Role playing social situations that children are likely to meet, such as those occurring at play or at lunch times. Asking questions about how people felt, what could have made things better.

☞ Giving children a verbal script to practice for some settings or activities before they actually happen e.g. taking a visitor around the school.

☞ Discussions about how to welcome children who will be arriving new to the school mid-term.

Circle work in the infant classroom

Circle work has become increasingly popular with teachers over recent years, and has the advantage that it is very popular with pupils too.

Several books have been written that cover the theory and provide lesson plans and activities for different age-groups.

Many of the activities are applicable to the infant class, and in fact most teachers will have been familiar with elements of circle work for many years. They may not, possibly, have been carrying out activities in such a structured or cohesive way. This section only gives a taster of the many benefits and opportunities that circle work provides.

What is circle work about?

Circle time involves activities that increase self-awareness, awareness of others, self-esteem, cooperation, trust and listening skills. It encourages cognitive skills, such as the ability to reflect, predict, question, evaluate, explain feelings, encourage others in a positive way, and to speak publicly. Circle work encourages an accepting attitude of others, and helps to develop openness and caring. It also meets some of the National Curriculum requirements in terms of Speaking and Listening.

Circle work sessions

Some teachers use daily circle time sessions and others less frequently. For a very young class each session should not last more than 10–20 minutes.

Each session takes place with all participants sitting facing each other in a circle, and begins and ends with a fun activity – a game. Sometimes early circle work sessions consist solely of games until the children become accustomed to what is expected of them. Then one or more new activities will be introduced which will focus on the intentions and plans of the session. Early work might include a focus on affirmation, awareness of others, listening skills, imagination, and the building of confidence and trust. Then work can begin on exploring feelings, empathy, and finally problem solving and conflict resolution. Although circle work can be used successfully in this way, much of its focus is proactive and preventative in intent. Circle work can function on a number of levels, but the earlier ones such as developing listening skills, confidence, etc. must be established first. Teachers and children will need to feel comfortable before attempting to work on conflict resolution and higher levels.

Some schools have taken on circle work as part of a whole-school policy.

Rules for circle work

A few rules are necessary for circle work to take place. These can be devised by the group or by the teacher. This gives the children a formal structure in which they can contribute equally. Typically these might include:

● listen without talking while others are speaking
● no 'put-downs' about other people, only 'push-ups'
● speak only for yourself
● everyone has the right to 'pass' (with an opportunity to contribute later)

Young children find it difficult to wait their turn to speak so a special object, such as a shell or teddy, may be passed from person to person. The one holding that object at any time is the only one allowed to speak.

Many activities are simple sentence stems that each child completes in turn. This avoids one child from dominating the talking. Examples of these that would focus on affirmation are:

- My name is ....
- My favourite animal/food is ....

For imagination and feelings :

- If I could change the world, then I would ....
- I feel happy/sad when ....
- It makes me angry when ....

Star of the day

This is a circle time activity to support the Star of the Day idea described earlier.

Here, one child sits in the centre of the circle and each child in turn makes a positive comment about that child. This may take the form of a sentence-stem, such as:

- I like .... because ....
- .... is good at ....

Some children find it hard to be complimentary, and so are given the chance to pass. They can have another opportunity to comment when they have heard a few examples and had time to think. Initially, young children will focus on physical attributes, and the teacher may need to do some work to help pupils find appropriate things to say.

For some infant classes, it might be better to use a sentence stem :

- .... can jump/run/smile.' etc.

These are particularly useful ways to include a child who joins the class later in the term, when friendship groups might already have become established.

Circle time can be fun

It is important that the sessions are enjoyable for pupils. Many activities are designed to ensure that this is so, even though the session may have a particular focus, e.g. children learning about each other. Learning about each other is an important precursor to the establishment of friendships. After all, many friendships, adult or child, are based on what people have in common. Children also develop less prejudices against people they get to know, especially when they discover that there are experiences that they share.

There are physical games, such as action mime and follow me games where certain pupils change places, e.g. all those with blue eyes/wearing red, that encourage awareness and observation. Some of these are particularly useful for shy children and those at the early stages of English language acquisition.

Within the circle, children can work for a brief time with the person sitting next to them, and find out one or two things that they have in common. It is useful to remember that some withdrawn children do have the necessary social skills, but need to transfer their use to new settings.

The use of a puppet has helped some particularly shy pupils to have a voice. They provide a comment much more readily on the puppet's behalf.

Problem solving

At the more advanced level, where problems are brought to the group by pupils, careful planning has to be done. Issues of confidentiality and the appropriateness of the circle as a forum need to be considered.

One child brings a problem/something that bothers them to the group. Each child then offers a suggestion:

- Would it help if ....?

A typical problem might be feeling lonely in the playground/that their handwriting was not neat etc. Children can come up with wonderful ideas! Some of these have been taken up by the whole school.

Some young children might have difficulties with these higher level activities and the approach might need to be modified. The teacher herself could generate a problem, e.g. not having time to water the plants herself, and ask the pupils for suggestions that might be helpful.

An affective education gives children a greater awareness of self, a sense of responsibility for themselves, and helps them to make good decisions in their lives. Circle work puts feelings and emotions on the agenda of an affective curriculum.

Summary

In order to participate as a member of a class, young children have to be able to share adult time, attention, and equipment with others. They also need to accept that others have needs and learn to wait their turn. In order to do this, they firstly need to feel positive about themselves, and about their position in the group. In addition children need to have the necessary skills to enable them to engage with others successfully.

CHILDREN ARE MORE LIKELY TO COOPERATE WHEN :

- they are not overtired, ill, or anxious about something
- they understand exactly what to do
- they have the skills to be able to do what is requested of them
- they feel good about doing what is requested of them
- their compliance promotes a positive self-image
- they feel that systems within the school ensure fairness, and know they will get their turn
- they feel supported by friends and family
- there is consistency in the way they are managed

CHAPTER 10

DEALING WITH CONFLICT

Even in the most well behaved classrooms there will inevitably be some conflict: all young creatures get into play fights and children are no exception. Most of the time this isn't serious and upsets are quickly over. Teachers often wisely choose to ignore minor incidents, keep a watchful eye from a distance, and give children the opportunity to sort things out for themselves. Children need to learn to resolve their differences and jumping in too soon may be counter productive. Conflict is part of everyday life and it is how we learn to deal with it that is important. It follows that some individuals will need to learn that there are alternative strategies, to practice these and to understand that they can make choices.

The importance of outcome The different stages of development seen in children in the infant classroom include differences in their level of 'moral' understanding. Most, however, will still be at the level at which rules are followed because 'Daddy or teacher says so and because you get into trouble if you don't.' Judgements about behaviour are seen much more in terms of eventual outcome than of intentions. It is unlikely that all children will have yet learnt to distinguish between following social conventions (we all have to hang our coats up on the pegs) and moral conventions (we must not hit other children in the playground). Some schools have helped children learn to differ by having 'Safety Rules' and 'Golden Rules' the latter emphasising the importance of kindness and cooperation.

GOLDEN RULES

Do be gentle - don't hurt each other.

Do be kind - don't hurt feelings.

Do be honest - don't cover the truth.

Do listen carefully.

Do look after property - don't damage things.

Do work hard - don't waste your time or
other people's.

SAFETY RULES IN SCHOOL

Please walk at all times in school.

Please follow the arrows when you walk up or down the stairs.

Please walk up or down the stairs past Purple and Blue class if you take a message.

Please sit on the benches in the hall if you come to school early.

Please go to your class at 9 o'clock.

Please hang your coat on your peg.

Many children will be modelling their social behaviour primarily on family norms and how they observe people interacting in their home environment. Internalisation of moral values is still at an early stage. As a young child's moral development is demonstrated through relationships with others, helping him to learn to deal with conflict so that there are positive outcomes all round is a useful step in internalising certain values about the process of relationships. In this way he will begin to take account of another person's feelings and perspectives as well as his own and start to develop greater reciprocity in his interactions: 'If I want to play with your football at breaktime then I must be prepared to lend you my ruler in class'. Most children come to this understanding as a matter of course; for others there will be the need for greater guidance.

Developing conflict strategies in circle time

(See also the relevant section in Chapter 9, 'Cooperation and the Group')

The very process of circle time in which everyone must listen to everyone else and each person has their turn is a sound basis for teaching skills for basic conflict resolution. It also enables much groundwork to be covered that can then be referred to in individual incidents. Circle work is particularly useful in that it removes the initial focus from individuals and poses questions to the whole group. Solutions then become the responsibility of everyone. Experienced infant teachers have been using this method for years although not necessarily in such a structured way.

The following is just one example of conflict resolution.

Defining the problem

'There have been a lot of children coming to the dinner helpers saying that some rough children have been knocking them over in the playground. Sometimes this has led to some fighting – we must think of what we can all do about this. First of all everyone think of why this might be happening, why people are getting knocked down:

- 'Sometimes people bump into others when..........'

'Why is this not a good thing to be happening in the playground?'

- 'Bumping into people makes them feel..............'

Finding solutions

To follow this up the circle could be asked what each could do:

- 'I could try not to bump into people by................'

For the following few days the teacher could remind the class of their good ideas before they go out to play. She could also have another circle time session to review how things are now.

Taking evasive action

Classroom management and resources

The source of frequent conflicts may be issues that can be easily dealt with by some rethinking about use of facilities and resources. Overcrowding in areas of the classroom, too many demands on equipment at one time or lack of clarity about roles and responsibilities may all engender conflict. Once the problem has been identified, asking pupils about resolutions could be a first step and helps them to learn about negotiation.

Individual children

Sometimes there are unhappy youngsters who come into school just spoiling for a fight. It is likely that things have happened at home which have made them unsettled. It is also possible that they may have had a late night and been rushed to school half awake, making them generally out of sorts. Although they would be ready to pick an argument with anybody, there are always some individuals who seem to be standing in the way.

A sensitive teacher may realise as soon as the day starts that evasive action will need to be taken. This may take the form of having a quiet word with the angry child to let him know that she is aware that he is feeling upset and maybe giving him some way of expressing this safely. Talking or pretend play or perhaps an activity which uses up some energy might all help. Joining another class for PE first thing in the morning could be a solution. Some children may benefit from five calming minutes away from the classroom with a sympathetic adult, such as a nursery nurse, perhaps having a drink and possibly something to eat. Teachers may also rearrange class groups for the morning or make sure that there is a more structured activity at playtime which minimises disputes. Discussions with parents which acknowledge the difficulties they may be experiencing but also look for some manageable solutions would be helpful in the longer term.

Avoid taking sides

There are times when minimal intervention by an adult is unavoidable to prevent conflict from escalating. Where one person is upset, some teachers have found that attending to that person and comforting them is a better strategy than giving attention to an aggressor. The difficulty with this strategy is that the child who is upset may, in fact, be the one who, out of the watchful eye of an adult, initiated the conflict and provoked a response – it may be better to avoid taking sides at all. A child who is frequently seen to be involved in conflict soon becomes labelled a troublemaker. The situation often then snowballs with assumptions being made whenever there is a dispute that this particular child is to blame and he quickly becomes a scapegoat. All staff in the school, including dinner supervisors, need to be aware of this danger.

Re-establishing harmony
Making small children say sorry to each other may not always be a very meaningful activity but there are other ways to re-establish some harmony.

☞ Suggest the children shake hands or give each other a hug – this may make them laugh. This won't work at the height of the conflict – the children may be asked to wait somewhere in separate places until they have calmed down.

☞ Tell them that they may say the following to each other in turn and the other has to listen.
- one thing about why they are upset
- one thing about what they would like the other person to do to make them feel better
- one thing that they will do to make amends.

No discussion is allowed, each child is given a short while to think about it and then come to an agreement. If no agreement can be reached the children try again at the next break, with as much guidance as they need.

☞ Give them both a task to do together, possibly at playtime, for which they can be rewarded if they carry it out responsibly. This gives both children the opportunity to apply positive labels to themselves and perhaps re-establish friendly behaviour during the activity. It may be better to wait until the day after the conflict to do this.

Figure 10.1 Sharing a task

☞ For fighting tell the children 'You two just wait here until I am ready to talk to you'. Ten minutes of wondering what is going to happen may forge a sense of identity and alliance which is stronger than their differences. The eventual question, 'What are you going to do to be friends again?' may be all that is needed.

☞ Do not always attempt to 'get to the bottom of things' – this is often time consuming and not always fruitful. Sometimes a situation does warrant further investigation or children need to feel they have been 'heard'; it will depend on the circumstances.

99

LIVERPOOL HOPE UNIVERSITY COLLEGE

Win/Win situations

One of the most useful things that children can learn from conflict situations is that there doesn't always have to be an outright winner and a loser. Children can be encouraged to develop the skill of looking for solutions and compromises by having this modelled by teachers and other adults in the school. One of the reasons that 'saying sorry' is used such a lot is because it somehow gives the impression that it evens things up.

Developing ways to help children to both think up ways of 'balancing' the fairness quotient and also responding to offers of negotiation is useful.

Disputes

☛ It helps children to handle disputes if they are encouraged to make 'needs' statements which clearly communicate what they want. Instead of saying: 'You're a pig, you never let me play', suggest the child says: 'I want to play in your game – can I?'. Instead of saying: 'I don't like you, you shout at me', say: 'I don't like it when you shout at me – I want you to talk to me properly'.

The same principle of 'win/win' can apply in disputes too. The following is an example of how to re-establish balance to ensure there is no outright winner or loser in a dispute. It also provides opportunities for positive feedback on pro-social behaviour .

Abdul accuses Billy of taking his ball. Billy denies this. Abdul is encouraged to make a 'needs' statement instead of blaming. He says: 'I just want my ball back'. Billy is asked by the teacher to think of at least five places it might be and to help Abdul look for it during this playtime and to ask three more people to help next playtime if it isn't found. Even if it doesn't turn up Abdul will be reminded that Billy has given up two playtimes in looking.

'I had it first!': The child who takes something that she wants when others are playing with it or about to use it can generate a conflict situation very quickly. It is, of course, better if children ask before they take something but it isn't always clear that this is necessary. If the class work out together, possibly in circle time, what the expectations and responses should be in this situation everyone can support each other is sorting out such disputes without teacher intervention. It takes away the personal threat and gives clarity. Similar strategies can be developed to de-escalate other potential conflicts. It may take some time for such strategies to become routine but they will do with practice.

Saving Face: Sometimes children feel that they lose face if they back down from a situation, perhaps a challenge to fight. It is useful if they can give reasons for doing this which are not threatening to their self-esteem.

☛ The class could brainstorm ways of saying 'No'
☛ Using an authority figure to resist peer pressure can also help: 'I'm not going to fight you because my mum doesn't like me fighting'.

Bullying behaviour

If conflict between children is disruptive to activities in the classroom or if one child is heavily intimidating another, then immediate adult intervention is necessary. There is evidence to suggest that when bullying behaviour is not addressed at an early stage then it continues and escalates as the child grows older. There is a danger that children come to feel that bullying others does meet some of their needs, e.g. for self-esteem or control. Much bullying behaviour is a result of poor social skills or low self-esteem.

The staff group need to decide what constitutes bullying – it isn't a straightforward concept. Most definitions, however, would include a deliberate use of power and threat to intimidate and undermine another child. When a child, or group of children, is seen to be bullying this should be taken seriously within the context of whole school policies both on behaviour and equal opportunities.

Make it very clear to all children (and all staff) which bullying behaviours are unacceptable in school. This is better presented as positive statements, e.g. 'In this school we will be kind to each other'. Such rules will need to be discussed with the children so that they have themselves thought about what it means to be 'kind'. Inclusion in games will need to feature here as active rejection can be just as damaging as aggression.

Teach all children to resist bullying behaviour themselves by simple assertiveness strategies. The simplest one is to teach them to say clearly and directly: 'Stop it, I don't like it' and then move away. Children can be encouraged to think in Circle Time of other phrases and the situations in which they would be appropriate. Some less confident children may need practice and support to develop and use these strategies. Helping children to learn simple assertiveness skills at an early age is empowering and will prove valuable to them throughout their school life.

☞ Teach all children to support and look out for each other against bullying behaviour.
☞ Actively discourage children from labelling someone as a 'bully'.
☞ The 'no-blame' approach is useful, especially where groups of children are involved: this is where no attempt is made to get to the root of an incident but the perpetrators of bullying behaviour are told that a certain child is feeling bad about some things which are happening in school. They are asked how they are going to help their classmate feel happy and safe. This is then monitored.
☞ Teach the child who is bullying others alternative ways of interacting which maintain their self-esteem.

Talk with parents, initially on their child's entry to school, then whenever the opportunity presents itself, to explain that smacking their children as a regular way of getting them to do as they are told, teaches them to use physical force in the playground and that this:

● gets their children into trouble and
● makes their children unpopular.

Parents may want to know about alternative ways of managing their children and this provides a good opportunity to develop home/school collaboration in developing positive behaviour management.

Chances to make amends

When one child is found to be intimidating another a graded response to such behaviour is helpful; this gives the child a chance to learn new behaviours but also gives teachers something to fall back on if the first strategies don't meet with success .

1. Deal with incidents first at an individual level with the class teacher talking with the child making it clear which behaviour is unacceptable. The child is expected to change their behaviour and either keep out of the other child's way or make an effort to be more friendly. They are given the choice. A review should be held to give positive feedback on success.

2. If the bullying behaviour continues the child should meet with the class teacher and another member of staff, possibly the Headteacher, where the seriousness of the matter is emphasised and consequences if it doesn't stop are explained.

3. The next step requires the use of consequences and sanctions within school.

4. More serious episodes of bullying necessitate the involvement of the parents of the child who has been bullying.

Although teachers might feel that they should contact parents immediately this is usually the sanction that has most impact with children and is therefore probably best saved until other ways of addressing the issue have been tried. It is important to discuss with parents the sanctions that would be appropriate. If the child feels bullied at home it may reinforce this behaviour in school.

Name-calling and teasing

Unkind words which threaten the self-esteem of individuals can be seen as verbal bullying and need to be addressed promptly. Using Circle Time activities and carpet time sessions would ensure that the whole class knows what is and what is not acceptable and is enabled to look at the feelings engendered by name-calling. It is important for infant teachers to be aware that some children simply don't know or realise that certain words are hurtful and this needs to be explained gently at first. The same applies to swear words. Some individuals put others down by name calling because it is a way of maintaining their own vulnerable self-esteem. Raising their self-esteem therefore needs to be part of interventions.

☛ As with other assertiveness strategies children can be encouraged to find statements to respond to name-calling such as: 'That's not funny', 'That's just silly'. Defensive statements such as 'I'm *not* stupid' are unhelpful as they maintain the interaction by highlighting negative labels.

The child who wants to dominate

The child who wants to throw his weight about, be first, have the last word, have everyone play games his way, needs to learn more socially acceptable and cooperative ways of behaving if he isn't going to get into conflicts on a daily basis. His peers are likely to give him guidance here but there needs to be constant reinforcement of expectations from teachers as stated in the chapter on cooperation. This child's popularity will increase if he is able to harness his extrovert nature to include other children. He can be encouraged to do this by saying, e.g. 'Let's....... ask John if he wants to play, make room for Monica, listen to what Omar is saying', etc. Children need to be able to identify their end goals and have an awareness that immediate goals may be in conflict with these. 'If you always push in, how do you expect people to want to be your friend and play with you?'

☞ Giving responsibility to children who want to be 'in charge' is another way of harnessing their particular energies. It addresses their self-esteem needs and can also give teachers opportunities to teach more appropriate 'leadership' skills.

Conflict with teachers

Those youngsters who are particularly immature or have not experienced consistent boundaries may find it hard at first when they discover that they don't always get their own way in school. Adults can use up a great deal of valuable energy in conflict with small children and wherever possible it is best to attempt to de-escalate confrontation. Awareness of personal 'flashpoints' and a calm and consistent response are not easy to maintain but are effective. A teacher who is regularly 'beside herself' with irritation and anger and shows this not only to the individual child but also to other children in the class may very well inspire fear but will not be able to establish the relationships that are necessary to effect any long term change.

It is helpful for all the class to see that the adult is in control of their own emotions and can model ways of handling difficult and provocative situations. Principles of negotiation and 'balance' apply equally to teachers as to the pupils. Wherever possible a lightness of approach, some gentle humour and a reinforcement of positive labels is a good way of showing that the adult is in control both of the situation and of herself. For example, a teacher who has already made concerted efforts to get children to apply positive labels to themselves could say with a smile:

● 'I just don't believe that my lovely helpful Darren is refusing to.....'
● 'What's all this about then? – it's not like you. You had such a good day yesterday. What's the problem?'
● 'You must be feeling cross with everything today.'

☞ Offering the child some way out of a confrontational hole they have dug themselves into may be useful. A limited choice is one way, e.g. 'Do you want to sit here and do nothing and have to miss your playtime or come out in the corridor to try and sort things out?' A face-saving solution is another: 'If you start to pick up some of the pencils you threw down I will come and help you with the rest'.

(See also the appropriate sections in Chapter 11, 'The Hard to Manage Child').

Summary

Conflict is inevitable at all ages – the sooner children learn a variety of strategies and ways to solve problems the more able they will be to manage conflict in the future. Young children need to be encouraged to work things out for themselves in ways which include clear communication, 'I' statements, fairness and a sense of balance. There is a need for quick intervention if children are bullying others, again with the emphasis on making amends. The teacher's role is vital in modelling calm ways of managing conflict and looking for solutions.

CHAPTER 11

THE HARD TO MANAGE CHILD

So far we have largely concerned ourselves with the promotion of positive behaviours within the infant classroom and looked at what might be done to prevent potential difficulties arising or escalating. This final section is intended to clarify concerns for teachers who continue to be worried about the behaviour of some individuals. Despite clear and consistent expectations, a warm and accepting approach and teaching of routines these are children who remain exceptionally hard to understand and manage. Although we naturally want answers to the question 'Why?', and knowing more about a child's situation often does increase understanding and empathy, it is not always necessary to know detailed reasons in order to begin to identify the child's needs and ways to go about meeting these. The ideas found in this chapter are not intended to replace what has already been said but to contribute to developing a closer focus on what is happening for the individual in difficulty.

All behaviour is open to change

This book has stressed throughout that whatever the aetiology of any behaviour difficulty, even if it is the result of unmet emotional needs or an innate condition, there is a learning component with which teachers and parents can work. Part of an individual programme might be to encourage the child to learn to think about himself more positively – or to learn that some adults will always do what they say they will do. The programme for each child and the extent to which behaviour can be modified will depend on many factors. This will include how significant people think about the difficulties and the extent and nature of their involvement. It may be that part of the 'subtext' of some programmes will be to 'reframe' the view that others have of the child and/or her needs.

The importance of consistency

Behaviour rarely changes overnight and the learning experiences of four or more years will not be turned around without time and patience. Teachers who claim to have 'tried everything' with a child and found that 'nothing works' may in fact have tried several different strategies for a short time only or only on the days when they remember. When different adults in the school have different approaches and expectations this will also be confusing to the child who gets mixed messages about what is expected in school. Most children do eventually learn to respond to consistent messages about 'how we do things around here'. A calm approach and a quiet reminder frequently and consistently carried out is likely to be much more effective in changing children's behaviour than more severe but less consistent reactions to incidents of unwanted behaviour.

Short term management and longer term change

We are concerned here with behaviour which needs to be managed so that the teacher can get on with the job of teaching but also needs to be changed so that the child can get on with learning. It is useful to be clear about which is the focus for any intervention. Short-term management strategies help teachers to cope with difficult behaviour as it is occurring in the classroom or playground. It is what you actually do at the moment when Ayse is crawling under the tables playing sea monsters instead of getting on with her number work, when Andrew has his hands over his ears and is screaming for his mummy, or when Demetrius has just torn up the work of the person sitting next to him.

It is very useful to discuss and agree what responses are acceptable within the context of the whole school so that individual teachers feel confident that their strategies will be understood and supported by their colleagues. These may or may not be part of a longer term promotion of behaviour change. For example, something needs to be done about the child – let's call him Danny – who habitually throws pencils, erasers etc., at his classmates. A short-term management strategy could be to put Danny on a table by himself. This may prevent him disrupting other children and teaches him what is not acceptable, but doesn't necessarily teach him new behaviours. Under the Code of Practice, a Stage Two target for Danny might be to learn to gain attention by positive behaviour. An individual programme to help him learn this might include the following:

- Give him his own special pencil with his name on it.
- A star or 'well done' sticker for each piece of completed work, graded so that he experiences early success.
- Regular praise for improved work and behaviour, by both his teacher and his mother, perhaps daily at first and then less frequently.

If this happens consistently over a period of time Danny will learn that:

- He gets great attention for behaving in the way his teacher wants him to.
- It feels good for important people to be pleased with him.
- His mum and his teacher are saying the same things to him and have the same expectations of his behaviour.
- Other children now want him to sit with them. (Though they might need to be told several times that 'Danny is learning not to throw things any more'. Small children are often very quick to tell the teacher about their classmates' misdemeanours – they can also be encouraged to 'tell' on progress).

Danny no longer gets an attention 'pay off' for throwing pencils and might begin to link working with pleasant emotions. It may be helpful if Danny's feelings about events are part of discussions and feedback so that he realises what makes him feel good. This will also promote the development of a language for emotions that may stand him in good stead when he wants to express feelings that are uncomfortable, sad or angry.

Stage two assessment of individual needs

The behaviour of any child is the outcome of many interacting factors, some of which are within the control of the teacher and others not. Teachers need to focus their thoughts and efforts on what is within their power to change. What we have done here is to develop a conceptual framework which places a behaviour primarily within one of several areas. This simplistic approach is deliberate in order to lessen the confusion which often characterises behavioural concerns in the classroom and to clarify the best way forward both for management and for meeting the child's needs. Although the child may be displaying behaviours that fit into several categories this process enables priorities to be made, 'next steps' identified and useful approaches clarified.

The areas we see as relevant and useful are as follows.

a. Behaviour as part of a learning or language difficulty i.e. the child is unable to follow instructions or understand what is expected and may be operating at a more immature level than others in the class. Some children's behaviour will be the result of frustration at not being able to communicate effectively.

b. Behaviour that stems from poor social interactions i.e. the child has not yet learnt how to go about playing and working cooperatively with others, gets into disputes frequently, pushes her way into games, misjudges others' intentions and gets into trouble frequently in the playground.

c. Disruptive behaviour i.e. the child may not be used to having consistent boundaries imposed and may find it very difficult at first when limits are placed on him in school. This child is also likely to have learnt that a reliable way of getting attention is to behave in ways that upset or irritate others, either peers or adults. Waiting for or sharing attention is also difficult.

d. Behaviour that is the result of inability to settle to work or respond to direction i.e. children who are a concern to teachers because they appear to be under-achieving: they flit from one thing to another, find concentration very difficult, are poorly motivated or very slow to respond to direction and do not complete tasks given. Care needs to be given to ascertaining whether this child has a learning difficulty, whether events outside school are absorbing the child's thinking or whether the child has a fear of failing. Sometimes such children are very impulsive and their difficult behaviour stems from this.

e. Behaviour that is extreme and accompanied either by a high level of emotion or with worrying 'blankness' i.e. something has happened, or is happening, to the child which is making them very distressed, angry, withdrawn or demanding. On investigation these children may have suffered serious lack of security, experienced the loss of a significant person, been a witness to violence or other trauma, or have been abused in some way. Children who have not had opportunities to develop a positive sense of themselves and have very low self-esteem would also fit into this category. They are some of the most difficult children to manage.

f. Behaviour which is particularly unusual i.e. any repetitive, obsessional, bizarre or socially inappropriate behaviour which may need to be investigated further. Children who are on the autistic continuum or who may have other conditions/syndromes may come into this category.

ACTION FLOWCHART

CHECK ISSUES THAT MAY BE CONTRIBUTING TO THE
CHILD'S ABILITY TO COOPERATE

HEARING, VISION, MEDICAL NEEDS
DEVELOPMENTAL ISSUES
LANGUAGE SKILLS
FACTORS AFFECTING THE CHILD'S SECURITY

IDENTIFY PRIORITY AREA(S) FOR INTERVENTION

LEARNING OR LANGUAGE NEEDS
SOCIAL INTERACTIONS
SETTLING TO WORK
GENERAL DISRUPTION
EMOTIONAL DISTRESS
INAPPROPRIATE /UNUSUAL BEHAVIOURS

MEET WITH PARENTS/CARERS AND OTHERS AS
APPROPRIATE TO DEVISE AN INDIVIDUAL
EDUCATION PLAN

CARRY OUT IEP CONSISTENTLY FOR A MINIMUM
OF 6 WEEKS
THEN REVIEW WITH ALL CONCERNED

DECIDE NEXT ACTION

Figure 11.1 Action flowchart

Stage two intervention and suggestions for action

The ideas that follow have worked successfully for some teachers with some children. We are very conscious of the demands on teachers in classrooms and most ideas involve different ways of doing things rather than additional things to do. There is often an incentive, however, to plan individual intervention because of the time it takes to respond every time the child is difficult. Some of the following ideas can be incorporated into individual education plans at Stage Two. Teachers should choose strategies with which they feel most comfortable, be consistent in their implementation and give them time to take effect.

A) LEARNING/LANGUAGE NEEDS
i) Learning difficulties

Many of the behaviour difficulties that present themselves in the classroom are linked to children's difficulty in understanding what is required of them or in their ability to do it, especially when given tasks which are beyond their capabilities. Further assessment may indicate that the child is very immature in her overall development and her behaviour is in line with this rather than that which may be expected of a school age child. Development may be delayed for many reasons including unmet emotional needs. More direct and structured teaching is needed where other children may learn 'incidentally' and more repetition is required to consolidate new skills.

- ☞ Re-gauge expectations and establish different approaches in the light of the child's overall functioning.
- ☞ The basic principles in teaching expected behaviour remain the same but there will be a need for much more repetition and reinforcement.
- ☞ Provide practical examples and concrete materials wherever possible.
- ☞ Some routines may need to be taught in smaller steps.
- ☞ Some routines may need to be taught individually or in a small group.
- ☞ Remember that the child is likely to still be in the egocentric phase of development for longer and behaviour management will need to take account of this; i.e. appeal to what is in it for the child to behave well rather than refer to the needs of others.
- ☞ Focus the child on imitating good models of behaviour but also maintain his self-esteem by structuring opportunities for him to show others 'how to'.
- ☞ Concentrate on a minimum number of 'rules' at a time and give concrete rewards for compliance where appropriate.
- ☞ Always refer to the actual behaviour and avoid using more abstract terms such as 'good' or 'naughty'.
- ☞ Assess understanding of basic classroom language and teach what is necessary for following instructions.

Poor response to direction   Children who are behaving more like a three year old than a five or six year old are more difficult to engage in teacher directed activities. Teachers have found the following helpful:

☛ Wherever possible build on what the child is already doing and interested in.

☛ Offer a choosing activity to follow a directed activity.

☛ If necessary keep directed activities short so that the child can experience success.

☛ Raise motivation and provide opportunities for success and praise by prompting: i.e. tell the child what you are going to ask the class to do in a minute so that they can be ready.

☛ Keep instructions very short and simple.

☛ Use gestures as well as words where possible to explain what is going to happen next.

☛ Always move closer to the child, coming down to their level physically and getting direct eye-contact when giving individual support or instructions.

☛ Ask the child to say in their own words what they are going to do next to ensure that they have understood.

☛ Refocus by using individual names.

☛ Give 'larger than life' specific praise for both effort and attainment – subtlety is less effective.

☛ Put the child in groups with children who are good models for behaviour, encourage him to copy them and then encourage these children to say positive things about how well everyone worked or played together.

☛ Keep the child close by, e.g. in 'carpet sessions' facing the teacher, so that the teacher can subtly refocus when attention wanders.

Immediate management strategies

☛ Give a moment of two for compliance focusing on praising children who are responding, especially those near the child.

☛ Repeat clearly but firmly what is expected and where appropriate either propel the child or take by the hand to the directed activity saying: 'Come on – I'll help you get started' – or ask a another child if they can do this.

☛ If the child objects restate firmly with smile: 'This is what we do in this class – you show everyone how well you are learning to sit down/be ready, how grown up you are' etc.

☛ Offer a distraction, e.g. 'You hold the book ready for me', 'You tell me who clsc is sitting nicely'.

☛ Sometimes it is helpful to get a child started on a task by physically doing things with them – an adult's hands over the child's hands – or making a game out of imitating.

☛ If the child is becoming increasingly negative, however, avoid initial confrontation – say you will come back in a minute to see how they are getting on.

☛ If on your return they are not complying use the strategies found in the section on 'disruptive children'.

Overexcitement

Sometimes young children's behaviour can deteriorate simply because they have become over excited about events. They may also become overtired more quickly.

☞ Calm the child down by holding both their hands and speaking quietly to them.

☞ Model deep breathing and encourage the child to copy.

☞ If several children are also in need of a quiet time play **'Sleeping Lions'** in which everyone lies on the floor and the teacher has to look for any movement for the child to be 'out'. Children who are 'out' must stay silent but can point to others who are moving.

☞ Some teachers have successfully used quiet, soothing music or relaxation tapes and techniques to calm down an overexcited class.

☞ Give the child a 'comfort cushion' to hold in a quiet corner.

☞ If the child is constantly crotchety check with parents how much sleep he is having. This is very important. Some parents don't realise how much sleep young children need if they are going to be alert enough to learn the next day.

ii) Language difficulties

Children who are experiencing a difficulty with communication frequently present with behavioural difficulties linked to frustration. By and large this applies to children with language delay or disorder rather than children who are in the early stages of learning English as a second language. Young children who arrive in school having only heard and spoken their own language tend to pick up English remarkably quickly unless there are additional difficulties. Although they are initially at a disadvantage this is usually short-lived especially where the teacher uses language in manageable amounts with visual and contextual support.

The strategies outlined here may be helpful for all children who need to develop language skills:

☞ Set the context for such children by using visual means and modelling to help them understand what they are supposed to do.

☞ Use and encourage body language, gestures and facial expression as an aid to communication.

☞ For some children miming can be helpful. As a 'fun' activity it can help to take the heat out of difficulties sometimes.

☞ Pay attention to the process of activities especially for older infants: i.e. give an interim non-language based task until the teacher is available to help, especially with routine tasks such as 'writing news'.

☞ Encourage watching and copying others.

☞ Teach the child to say: 'I don't understand' or 'I don't know what to do' and welcome this when they come for help.

☞ Encourage expressive communication by vocal, verbal, gestural and visual means.

☞ Be patient when a child is trying to communicate something. Repeat what you think the child said and ask them 'Is that right?'

☞ Ask the child to help you understand by saying it another way or showing you.

☞ Ask another child to help – they may understand better than you can.

☞ Encourage the child to speak slowly, directly at the listener and not to obscure their mouth with their hands

Figure 11.2 Children don't always understand every word you say

☛ Where children have articulation difficulties parents are often able to assist the teacher in picking up clues to help decipher what is being said.

☛ 'Story time' needs to be short and supported by pictures and 'larger than life' gestures. If children's attention is constantly refocused onto the story in such a way the less opportunity there will be for getting up to mischief in corners!

☛ Listening skills can be enhanced if some children are asked to look out for certain characters or objects in the story and make a signal, e.g. a clap or a hand up, every time they are mentioned, a bit like booing at the wicked witch in a pantomime!

☛ A whole class was taught some basic Makaton sign language for one child who was having a severe difficulty with language. The children really enjoyed this and it gave that particular child far more routes into social communication and therefore involvement in the class than had been previously possible. The child was also 'the expert' for once which raised his self-esteem.

Immediate management strategies

☛ When a child's frustration has reached a peak give him something to do which takes up physical energy or where he can easily be successful until he has calmed down.

Language and literacy

Many children who are delayed in acquiring language often have difficulty acquiring literacy. Even if a child has learnt to communicate satisfactorily they may still have poor auditory skills. If a child has a problem with **I-spy** games or rhymes and difficulty remembering auditory information then they will need special attention in developing reading skills with an initial emphasis on visual skills, i.e. learning a small sight vocabulary of highly meaningful, easily discriminated words such as 'dinosaur' or 'teddy'. Phonics can then be built on words they can already read. Many children referred for behaviour difficulties in later years have struggled to maintain their self-esteem in the face of failure with basic academic skills. In the end it may be safer not to try and to seek status in their peer group in other ways.

B) SOCIAL INTERACTIONS

Some children are forever getting into arguments and fights. They seem unable to play happily with their peers, unless those children are particularly passive and willing to be dominated. Other children come constantly to adults to complain of bullying, unfairness and 'spoilt' games. Within a working context these children experience difficulties in collaborating effectively. They can be aggressive, demanding and are frequently 'in trouble', especially at playtimes and dinnertimes. For some children who have not had the experience of secure and trusting relationships this behaviour may make sense to them. They need to learn that other social behaviours are possible and can be effective in getting their needs met. They also need to learn to trust people in school which is far more demanding, especially when their behaviour invites rejection. Other children who have social difficulties may simply not have learnt the behaviours that enable them to establish and maintain friendships. They may have been encouraged to 'stand up for themselves' at all costs or had doting parents for whom they could do no wrong. Coming to school may be the first experience of 'social realism' for these children who need to become 'socialised' in ways that help them become a successful and happier member of the class group. These skills can be summarised as:

- gaining entry into group activities
- including others in games – sharing and turn-taking
- being supportive and approving to other children
- managing conflict in an appropriate way.

Intervention for individual children with social difficulties is rarely sufficient. By the time an individual programme is put into place the rest of the class are very likely to have 'labelled' the child concerned – and so might their parents. Work needs to take place to change the perceptions of everyone in this situation as well as developing skills for the individual child. Discussions of whole class work to develop collaboration are found in Chapter 9, 'Cooperation and the Group'.

Figure 11.3 Some children need to learn the skills to play with each other

Individual skill development

Although many of these strategies can be applicable to the whole class it is the structure and detail of the focus for the individual here which is important. Sometimes children whose pro-social behaviour is underdeveloped need to learn actual behaviours, both verbal and non-verbal, for specific situations. They may need to practice these within a small group with and without supervision and the links should be made to enable these learnt skills to generalise to less structured situations in the playground and classroom. The teaching of skills needs to go hand in hand with facilitating age appropriate social understanding, especially the need for rules, and reciprocity.

☞ 'Catch the child being friendly' – make comments to highlight the specific behaviour that is socially appropriate and link the situation to positive feelings for the child.

☞ Structure situations which enable you to comment positively on individual actions e.g. ask a child to show someone where something is – or how to do something .

☞ Encourage children to look friendly. Good eye contact and smiling really is very helpful – children avoid others who moan, whine and look grumpy all the time.

☞ Give guidance and daily opportunities to 'help' others including making space, joining in games, lending etc.

☞ Encourage the child to be aware of others, make positive comments and show interest. Children with difficulties need to be guided by the teacher in this, e.g. 'I see that Michael has returned to school – why don't you go and say "Hi" and ask him why he was away?', 'Ellie has just had a new baby sister – I wonder what her name is – can you find out for me?' If you do this before a carpet session this friendly behaviour can be mentioned to the group.

☞ Teach the child to ask: 'Whose game is it?' and ask that person if they can play – or just ask 'Can I play?' Other children will need to be taught that the answer to this question always has to be 'yes', even if there are conditions attached.

☞ Teach turn-taking and sharing in a graded way, beginning with a supervised pair until the child can manage in an unsupervised group and generalise skills to a variety of contexts.

- When it comes to less structured 'turns', such as time using a computer, make sure the child knows when it is their turn and when their turn will be finished. Give warning of activities coming to an end. It is useful to match this with a 'natural break' such as playtime or dinner time this avoids possible conflict when the turn is finished.
- Structure paired work so that each child has a clearly identified role and task. Praise is given for collaborative skills as well as the product.
- Remind the child of at least one social skill they have been learning before going out to play.
- Work on perceptions and the assumptions the child makes, e.g. 'Could Jimmy have bumped into you by accident? – how can you tell?'
- Relate feelings to actions, e.g. 'You had a great game with Leo this playtime – I bet you feel good about that.'
- Raise the child's self-esteem by public acknowledgement of strengths and progress, especially with regard to behaviour development.
- In one school adults take a small group of children and act out some social situations, such as wanting a toy someone else is playing with. They begin by showing inappropriate behaviours in a 'larger than life' way which the children usually find very funny. The adults then talk about why that behaviour wasn't helpful and ask the children to suggest other ways of doing things. They then act out to the children's direction before asking the children themselves to practice.

Immediate management strategies

Pushing into a game, being rejected and reacting with anger

- Put the child's feelings into context and help them to verbalise them: 'You feel upset because they wouldn't let you play – is that right?
- Ask 'What would someone have to do to join *your* game?'
- For some older or more able children this could be reinforced by a drawing exercise – perhaps a page divided into four to represent the sequence of events.
- Ask 'What will you do next time?'
- Remind the child of this next time they go out to play.

Mild aggression in the playground

- The 'football card' system has been very successful. A child who is seen to be verbally or physically aggressive (pushing, shouting, etc) is given a yellow card. The 'third card' is a red card and they have to leave the playground and cannot come out to play the next playtime. As in football, this has to be adult observed behaviour not based on tales from other children. No excuses allowed!
- If a child's behaviour in the playground has been particularly difficult for other children and he loses his playtime as a consequence he can 'win' it back by being allowed out for increasing amounts of time. It may be better for this to be the last five minutes, ten minutes etc., which is more likely to give him a chance of success. An immediate public acknowledgement back in the class will help other children to be more accepting.

☞ Keeping children in and not giving them an outlet for pent-up energy may cause further difficulties. Finding ways that use up physical energy may be important for some.

(For Disputes, Domination and Bullying see Chapter 10 on 'Dealing with Conflict'.)

C) DISRUPTIVE BEHAVIOUR

This term has been used to separate this behaviour from that seen in children whose behaviour is driven by distress although what they actually do may be similar. In this context this term applies to children who seek attention by behaviour which is difficult to ignore, push boundaries to the limit or appear to take little notice of adults until they are at least at the shouting stage. They are likely to have learnt that adults take notice intermittently, say one thing one day and another the next, tell them 'no', but then 'give in' for a quiet life.

All children need attention – it is necessary for their survival. 'Attention-seeking behaviour' has developed negative connotations when in fact it is more appropriate to talk about 'attention needing'. Unfortunately many adults fail to learn that for most children, any attention is better than no attention. By the time they are four or five years old, children have often realised that attention will be immediately forthcoming, very focused and direct, *not* if they play quietly until supper time but if they make a right nuisance of themselves. This is behaviour that isn't so much dangerous as irritating – and may prevent the child from learning effectively. It is not always a conscious decision on the child's part to seek attention in this way but it may have become the way in which he has learnt to relate to other people. The expectations are that he will eventually get what he wants if he makes enough fuss and that an adult's 'no' will waver in time just to get some peace. Gaining the attention of classmates may also be a priority, regardless of where, when and how.

It requires a very high level of consistency and clarity to change this way of operating. This involves a graded response which initially gives maximum attention for acceptable behaviours and takes minimum notice of minor wind-ups, silliness and so on. Any positive reinforcement of wanted behaviour has to happen immediately. It isn't very meaningful to small children to have to wait until the end of the week, or even the end of the day, and often the adult's response has to be 'larger than life'. Involving parents in programmes will make a great difference both so that they can understand what is needed and also so that they can be encouraged to give positive attention rewards themselves as this is what their child is likely to value most. It is, however, essential that parents do not feel pressured into offering rewards if they are not going to be able to deliver. It is better not to make promises than make them and break them.

Behaviour which continues or escalates should be addressed in the way outlined below under 'choosing the consequences'.

Promoting positive attention

☞ **'Catch the child being good'** – give positive reinforcement whenever the child is behaving in the way the teacher requires.

Figure 11.4 'Catch the child being good'

This can be graded according to the child's needs and progress and in ways that are most rewarding to the child. The children with the most difficulty with need a mix of all of these:

● a smile, a pat on the back or a thumbs up sign
● verbal attention, private praise
● public praise, larger than life attention
● stickers, hand stamps, badges, certificates.

Figure 11.5 Reward stickers, badges or hand stamps

☞ Where children are learning to wait for teacher time some intermediate attention by a positive comment is useful – the teacher could also say something like 'be with you soon.'
☞ **Star chart:** For children who need stronger reinforcement a 'star chart' can be very effective. This means that the most irritating behaviour is identified and then a decision made about what you want the child to do instead, e.g. putting a hand up rather than shouting out. Every time the child does this he is given a star or smiley face sticker. This chart can be

extended so that the five fingers of a hand represent five days. This reminds the child what he has to do and shows him how he is improving. Accumulative charts mean that for every five small stars the child wins a large star. For every five large stars a further reward is given e.g. a letter home, a special certificate in assembly, a more tangible reward either at school or at home. This method, when used consistently for several weeks, is very effective in developing specific behaviours but behaviour overall often improves as the child's self efficacy develops. It needs, of course, to be properly introduced with clarity about how long it will be in operation. If the child would like the star chart in a public place then other children need to be told that 'This is how we are helping ....to learn..............' Often other children will ask if they can have one too!

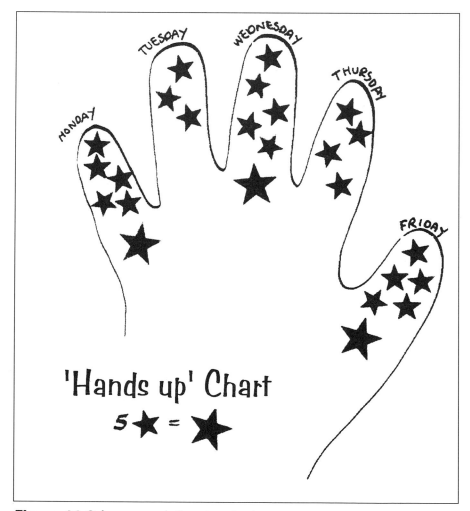

Figure 11.6 An accumulative star chart

Lee Cantor's Assertive Discipline strategies are useful for promoting positive behaviours. Bill Rogers' Behaviour Recovery strategies are also helpful in working with individual children to identify their own behaviour and the changes they need to make.

Giving minimal attention

In some families it is normal for shouting to be the signal for others to really take notice. Children therefore learn:

- not to comply with requests until then
- that they also have to make a fuss to be heard/noticed/gain attention.

Although bad behaviour cannot be 'ignored' as such – children need to know it is not acceptable – it should not be reinforced by high level, emotionally laden attention. The following is a suggestion about how to go about doing this in a graded way.

☞ Plan A:

- Praise children in the immediate vicinity for the wanted behaviour.
- Say something like: 'Isn't it strange that I can't hear someone when they are shouting/whining/interrupting – but I can when they put their hand up/wait so I can see they need me'.
- Make minimum eye-contact.
- The 'back in a minute' strategy for children can be very useful in some circumstances and gives the child a moment to make a choice about altering their behaviour. Many children will respond to teacher requests if they are given time to do so. A demand to 'do it now' may sometimes escalate a difficulty unnecessarily. Giving a child an instruction, for instance, to tidy away their toys may result in little immediate response, especially if the child is engrossed in what they are doing. If the teacher then says: 'I'll come back in a minute and see how you have got on', this gives the child some space to comply and doesn't take up undue teacher time and energy.
- If the child then conforms to the acceptable behaviour the teacher gives immediate eye-contact and a positive comment.

☞ Plan B:

- Say in a firm but calm voice: 'I am not going to shout at you but I expect you to ....'
- Coming up to children to speak to them quietly rather than calling out across the room is more effective.
- Speak as little and as quietly as possible to the individual concerned.
- Maintain a bland facial expression.
- Do not engage in lengthy conversation in which the child demands answers to the question 'why?' if it is another way of prolonging attention.
- The broken record: the teacher calmly restates expectations several times (whilst also attending to children who are behaving well) until the child shows some sign of altering their behaviour at which point they praise the child for the smallest amount of conformity.
- If the child continues to misbehave then more overt action is necessary.

☞ Plan C:

- Consequences: 1) A consequence for compliance which implies a consequence for non-compliance, e.g. 'When you've tidied up your toys you will be able to able to go out to play/come with us into assembly/have a tick on your chart.'

- Consequences: 2) When the child takes no notice of this then they need to know the consequences of their behaviour. It is useful if, where possible, consequences are linked with the misdemeanour, e.g. tell the child that if they are choosing not to work in lesson time, then they are *choosing* to work in playtime. At playtime they will be expected to work – the teacher should avoid all other conversation. It is essential that the consequence is one that is appropriate, manageable and that it will be carried through. Whatever the child then says or does should make no difference. Some children will become quite intimidating and throw a wobbly; some will get tearful; others will get into defensive arguments: 'Why me? It's not fair!'; others may now promise the world. It follows that offering a severe consequence in the first instance leaves you with nothing to fall back on. Look at graded sanctions in the way that you might look at graded rewards. Consistency, however, is more effective than severity if the same thing happens *every* time the child behaves in a certain way and this is something the child would prefer not to happen.
- The school's support system for managing behaviour should make it clear when it is appropriate for a child to be sent to the Headteacher and what response the Head will give to that child. It would be a mistake to send an attention demanding child to a situation where they may get rewarding undivided attention from an adult or attract the attention of other children in the corridor outside.

Immediate management strategies

☛ Counting: Many parents and teachers have found that young children often respond to the phrase: 'I'm going to count to three and I want it done by the time I get there ....1...........2......'. Children have often started to comply by the time you get to 3, but its a good idea to say each number slowly: 'ooonnnnne, twoooooooo' etc! This also adds some lightness to the situation. You could add the consequence for non-compliance if that is appropriate but it isn't always necessary. Alternatives to this strategy are numerous, e.g. 'by the time I've sung a nursery rhyme', 'by the time I've opened my eyes', 'by the time the sand has run through this timer', and so on. Using this strategy with a small group gives support to a child who might be having difficulty – the activity is redefined as 'fun' and they want to join in.

☛ The paradoxical instruction: Tell the child that if she wants to scream/whine then go ahead but it won't get her what she wants. Giving children permission to do something which is of its nature rebellious tends to take the steam out of it! It is also reassuring for the child that they are unable to manipulate an adult. This is only really useful if there is somewhere where other children won't be overly disturbed – it is unlikely to be effective in a small classroom, although even then it might be worth trying once! Other adults in the vicinity need to know the purpose of this or it can be misinterpreted.

☛ One teacher taught her entire class to look down whenever a child was behaving in a way which would be reinforced by their attention.

☛ This same teacher made herself a badge with 'Not Now Jason' written on it. Whenever the child in question interrupted her yet again all she had to do was tap the badge, without so much as looking at him. Eventually he learnt that he would get attention at more appropriate times, not on demand.

If there is an element of emotional distress for the child then additional strategies will need to be considered.

D) SETTLING TO WORK

Children who do not seem to able to listen, whose concentration span seems no longer than a few seconds, who are always out of their seat and never where they should be and who rarely finish what they start – if they start at all – are some of the most wearing to teach. They are often children who are also wearing to parent. In recent years there has been increased media coverage given to 'attention deficit disorder' which focuses on 'within-child' innate difficulties for which medication is advocated. This should be treated with extreme caution. There are many reasons for children's difficulties in concentrating. One is that attention difficulties are part of other problems, such as language delay, another is fear of failing, a third is that they have other things on their mind, and lastly they may never have been given the opportunity to develop and practice the skill of beginning, continuing with and finishing a set task. They may not even fully realise that there is an 'end goal' for some of the activities that they have been given unless this is made clear at the start. For some children the concept of 'finished' may mean when an adult says 'stop'. Small children are usually lively, mobile creatures and often unable to concentrate on one thing for long unless it is particularly fascinating to them. Gaining their interest, or using material which is directly relevant and of interest to them is a good place to start. Only when a range of possibilities have been explored and strategies tried and tested over a period of time is it relevant to start thinking about referral to doctors.

Getting started

☛ The timing of the day is important when considering which activities to do.
☛ Wherever possible plan an area with minimum distraction i.e. away from the door or window or active area. Specially arranged 'cubby-holes' or 'workstations' using bookcases or room dividers can be quite comforting as well as conducive to promoting work habits.
☛ Gain the child's visual attention before speaking to them. Give one piece of information at a time. Ask them to repeat the instruction in their own words.
☛ Make sure that the child has all the equipment they need and doesn't have to keep getting up to fetch things. Some teachers have put silhouettes of equipment taped to a table so that a child knows what they need.
☛ Sometimes extending activities that the child is already doing is a way of getting them used to direction.

- If a child is clearly distressed it is better to give them something that they can already do rather than expect concentration on something new.
- Don't give wide choices of activity. Where necessary limit choices to either/or. Ensure the child has told you what they have chosen before you leave them to get on with it. The inability to make decisions can result in flitting from one thing to another.

Staying on-task

- Whole class expectations about moving around the room need to be considered.
- Pretend to put special glue on the child's seat – they can only be 'unstuck' with the teacher's special words or wand!
- Manageable targets – start where the child is, with what they can do and build on this.
- At first give the child a very simple task in which they will be able to be successful, praise them for their ability to do it and reward them in some way – perhaps by an activity of their own choosing. Increase the length and complexity of the given task gradually.
- Some tasks could be pictorially represented in a simple sequence of steps. The child can tick off each step they complete. For children who are beginning to read a few words can also be added. Work can be done in pairs so that children support each other in staying on task.
- For some children work on sequences generally will be important – talking about what comes first, next and so on. This will need to be related to order in their own lives at first, e.g. the order in which they put their clothes on, the structure of the day and so on.

Task completion

- Make sure the child knows when a task is complete. It is frustrating for them to have to go back time after time because their idea of 'finished' is not the same as the teacher's.
- Let the children 'be the teacher' and put a smiley face on their complete work with a special pen.
- Structure 'personal best competitions'. Make sure that the child knows which target he is aiming to beat e.g. how many sums, the detail in a drawing, a decrease in the number of times he gets out of his seat etc.
- 'Record-breakers'. Give certificates, 'medals', etc., to take home for measurable targets.
- Use visual recording of success (bar charts, graphs, marbles in a jar) plus reinforcers and tangible rewards.
- Focus only on work completed or in-seat behaviour – don't ask for accurate, lengthy or beautifully presented work.
- Use an egg-timer or a stop watch so that children can monitor themselves. Larger timers are available in many school maths kits. Young children have an immature concept of time and this will need to be visually presented.
- Making 'I can' books generates more positive labels for children who find it difficult to take responsibility for both their attainments and their difficulties.
- Give children who have high levels of energy structured opportunities to 'let off steam'.

121

LIVERPOOL HOPE UNIVERSITY COLLEGE

☞ Work with parents to complete things at home, e.g. not leaving their place before others have finished a meal.

☞ Check with parents if there are foods which appear to make the child more active – there is evidence that some additives can exacerbate difficulties.

Immediate management strategies

● Ask the child if they know what they are supposed to be doing
● Ask them if they know how to do it
● Ask them what is the first thing they have to do
● Ask them to show you
● If the child does not know what to do then ask other children to show him and then ask him to copy
● Praise both efforts and attainments.

Impulsive behaviour

☞ Focus on the fact that the child can make positive choices. This is a particular form of positive reinforcement. For every time he is observed to be playing or working cooperatively he needs to be told: 'I see you have chosen to finish your picture, build a garage with Micah, do three sums today, etc.' Whenever the child acts impulsively he needs to be told: 'I see you chose: not to think about what would happen when/to stay in to finish your work/to spoil Joey's picture.' You could also prompt him by saying: 'What do you think is going to happen now?' If he says something like: 'Get told off' you may need to extend this to 'Joey won't want to sit near you or be your friend'.

As children get older they can be encouraged to become aware of their feelings in certain situations and how these feelings lead to certain actions. This could be the first step in developing a 'thinking gap' between impulse and action.

E) EMOTIONAL DISTRESS

It may be useful for this section to be read in conjunction with the section on emotional development in Chapter 2. Although many children may experience distress from time to time, this particular category is for children who are behaving in a way which indicates that they have little control over their emotions and that these are overwhelming them. For children who are expressing themselves by crying and/or screaming this distress will be obvious. It is less obvious for children who are hitting out with no apparent reason, who are destructive or who verbally abuse anyone who comes near. Children like this can be very upsetting to have in the classroom, partly because of the difficulty in managing their behaviour but also because their anger, confusion and misery often transfers to those working with them. It can be helpful for teachers to reflect that the feelings they have about a particular child may very well be the feelings that the child has about himself and the world. There are many reasons for children to be in this state. The most likely are:

- Family trauma – the child may be aware of emotional distress within the family but no-one will necessarily be talking to them about it. This makes children highly anxious. They may be imagining all sorts of things which might, in fact, be worse than the reality.
- Exposure to anger and conflict – this has an impact on children's emotional development and may make them tense, anxious and aggressive. They may work out their own feelings in school by repeating scenes that have happened at home.
- Family breakdown or bereavement – small children are much more affected by such events than is often realised. They often believe that it is in some way their 'fault'. They may be frightened that other important people will also leave. If a parent figure leaves and is unreliable about seeing the children then this can develop feelings of distrust as well as insecurity. Anger is part of a grieving process but children do not have the experience to help them to understand this. They do not know why they feel the way they do and this in itself can be confusing and upsetting. Some children express their anger at school because it is a 'safer' place to do so than at home. They may also be highly protective of those closest to them and not want to add to their worries by showing that they are upset.
- Emotional unavailability of a significant person – sometimes parents are so distressed by what is going on in their own lives they are unaware or unable to meet their children's emotional needs. A parent who is seriously depressed will be similarly cut off from their children. Often there is another important person in the child's life who can respond to them in the way that they need but where this is not the case then that child will themselves be highly distressed as some of their basic needs are not being met. Such children are also likely to be withdrawn or have a high level of attention seeking behaviour.
- Physical, emotional or sexual abuse – all teachers are aware of the possibility that they may have abused children in their class. Physical abuse is usually more easily detectable than sexual or emotional abuse but all are very upsetting when discovered. The behaviour of children suffering abuse, however, is a good clue to what is happening. They have difficulties expressing their emotions, show a higher than expected level of disregard to other people's feelings and may be very aggressive or withdrawn. Children who indicate inappropriate sexual knowledge either by behaviour or language need very careful monitoring. When emotional abuse takes the form of a level of control which means that the child is constantly criticised or punished for what may be normal curiosity, accidental behaviour or developing independence then the child may either be reluctant to try anything in school or attempt to exert control in a way that is not helpful.

In most of the above cases the self-esteem of the child is likely to be very vulnerable and raising this needs to be a major focus of intervention. The child needs to learn that they are likeable, are able to learn and that they can make choices for themselves. There are many ideas for this which can be adapted for individuals in Chapter 9, 'Cooperation and the Group'.

Being overwhelmed by feelings and being 'out of control' may be alarming for young children. It will help them to recover more quickly if the adult engaged with the child stays calm, acknowledges feelings, keeps talking to a minimum until there is some sign of recovery and offers physical comfort at an appropriate moment. If the child needs restraining, which may occasionally be the case, keep this to a minimum and at every point offer the child a choice to reassert control, i.e. 'Can you go to outside the classroom on your own or shall I take you?'

Many interventions to meet children's emotional and behavioural needs are dependent on the quality of the child's relationship with the teacher. The development of such a relationship may have a downside for teachers as emotionally distressed pupils may 'test out' trust and push boundaries. Carl Rogers talks about the need for 'unconditional positive regard'. This coupled with consistency, firmness and fairness is a high expectation of teachers. Whole school support is essential. *(See the section on 'The Network of Support ' in Chapter 5, 'The Needs of Teachers'.)*

Emotional distress: suggestions for action

Working with parents

☛ Talk with parents/carers about children's emotional needs. Explore with them how these might be met – what is realistic, who can help and support? It is very important not to attribute blame in these discussions – parents probably feel bad enough already. Even where you suspect abuse is happening putting parents on the defensive doesn't help anyone. Where you know it is happening then other professionals must be involved. In many cases parents may need reassurance about the skills they do have and given positive reinforcement for 'good enough' parenting in situations which would probably test anyone.

☛ Where events are home are difficult, such as separation or bereavement, encourage significant people in the child's life to talk to them at a level they can understand about what is happening. It is much worse for children to be excluded from important things in their lives, even if this is distressing for the adults.

☛ Let adults know how damaging it can be if children are pulled between two parents when there is a breakdown in the relationship. Ideally it is usually better for the child to maintain contact with both parents but not if they are used as pawns in a continuing battle or if they are not safe. If possible encourage an 'absent parent' to only make promises that they will keep.

☛ Parents who are experiencing difficulties with management at home may value some support from a child and family consultation service or possibly the NSPCC: it is far better if they come to the decision to make the referral themselves. Parents are unlikely to jump at the chance the first time the possibility is mentioned but might at some later stage.

Working with children

☛ Give children opportunities to express emotions safely – with trusted adults, in play situations, drawing, modelling, puppets etc

☛ **Traffic lights:** Some children have made indicators for teachers which show that they need help to manage their feelings. A green light means 'I feel OK', an orange one means 'I need some help soon', and red means 'I'm finding it really hard – please help now'. This is a way of helping children to begin to have some self-control. A record chart may be an additional way of identifying antecedent factors for the child.

☛ There are some excellent story books for children now available which deal with some of the difficult issues that children may be facing. These can be used with individual or small groups in the class to stimulate discussion about feelings and to show children that they are not all alone in their situation. A list is given in the reference and resources section.

☛ Teach children the language of emotions. For many young children there is real confusion between feelings of sadness and anger. If they can express what they feel in words there will be less need of fists.

☛ Without ignoring the difficulties encourage children to acknowledge the positive – I feel happy when.................

☛ Provide a constant, consistent, positive environment in which the child is reassured of his worth.

☛ Show warmth to the child by smiling and, if appropriate and welcomed by the child, physical gestures. This can include a quick hug, a tap on the shoulder, or a hand on the head.

☛ Whereas some young children need overt praise, emotionally damaged children find it more difficult to accept because it doesn't fit in with their concept of themselves. Positive comments need to be very specific indeed and given more privately. It is also useful to ask the child himself whether he thinks he did better on something. If he cannot see this, point out why it was better than before. This can be linked to either work or behaviour.

☛ Speak positively about the child to others in the child's hearing and encourage parents to do the same.

☛ Small children find it hard to believe that people who tell them off can still like them. Emotionally distressed children who have a low self-esteem will be particularly vulnerable and need reassurance that they are likeable and valued especially when being reprimanded. Stress the behaviour that is unacceptable and say something positive about the child himself.

☛ Young children pay most attention, not to the words, but to the emotional expression in language, i.e. the tone of voice, the loudness, the pitch etc. It is important that teachers are aware of this so that they give the messages they intend to give when speaking to children who are emotionally vulnerable.

Continue to have clear, consistent behavioural expectations as this will reinforce feelings of security for the child. Letting children 'get away' with things because they are upset isn't helpful.

Immediate management strategies:

☛ **Screaming/crying:** Acknowledge the child's distress. Take the line of least resistance and make no attempt to change the behaviour: 'I can see you are really upset – you have a good cry now', 'That's a very angry person screaming like that – you must be feeling terrible'. You could direct the child somewhere where there is less audience, such a medical room with a welfare assistant. You could add: 'Let me know when you

Figure 11.7 Even very young children can learn to offer each other emotional support

feel better and want to join the rest of our class'. You could mention something interesting the child would like to do when she comes back. You could offer physical comfort: 'Would a cuddle help?'. The child may yell 'no' in which case say: 'Well if you change your mind come and touch my arm to let me know'.

☞ **Difficulty in separating:** If a child is very clingy to a parent it may be useful for the parent to find something for him to hold who will 'help look after' him until 'mummy comes back'. This 'transference' object could be anything from a teddy to a handkerchief or piece of blanket. The teacher will need to find a place for the object when the child has had enough of holding it! This strategy is also useful for a child who is anxious about things happening at home. A mother may need to be encouraged to reassure her child that she will be all right – perhaps by telling him something she is looking forward to in the day.

☞ **Destructive behaviour:**

a) Own work: This is indicative of very low self-esteem. The child is literally 'rubbishing' themselves. The teacher's opinion at this moment may not have much impact. It is best to say: 'I'm sorry you feel like that about your work', or 'Maybe this isn't the best time to be doing this (activity), you can have another go tomorrow. Perhaps you won't be feeling so cross with yourself then'. Offer the child a practice activity or something else which is comforting to them and where they can be successful.

b) Constantly rubbing out. Tell the child that she cannot use the rubber at the moment because she is wearing it out! Suggest she has three goes on three bits of paper and choose the best. Explain that it's okay to make mistakes – everyone does, including the teacher.

c) Others' work: This is more likely to be indicative of unfocused anger. Give attention first to the child whose work has been damaged. Remove the angry child to a different part of the classroom. You could suggest that she makes something out of a big lump of plasticine that she can then be angry with, squash and remake. She might also like to make something for the child whose work she destroyed to show she is sorry. Children who are upset by their own impulsive outbursts may welcome this opportunity. Talking with her about this at playtime may help the child to understand a bit more about her feelings and the teacher to understand what is underlying her behaviour. There are other activities which may also serve to express some angry feelings – tearing up paper for papier-mache for example.

☛ **Aggressive outbursts to other children:** Make it clear to the child that their behaviour is not acceptable in school. Ask how they will make the other child feel better.

Don't ask the child 'why' he is behaving in the way he is – he is unlikely to know the answer and you may get a spurious reason. It is more helpful to ask: 'What were you thinking about when you did that?' It is best to do this at a later time rather than when the child is upset.

Time out: The child who is losing control may need somewhere to recover. Some classrooms have a special place where there is little distraction and minimum attention is paid to the child until he has calmed down. Children are encouraged to reassert self-control but this may be a staged process as follows:

- The teacher decides who goes to 'time out' and when they may return to the group
- The child is asked to 'Sit there and give me a signal when you are ready to work' This signal needs to be clear to both child and adult, e.g. arms folded.
- Children decide for themselves when they need time out.

Talk with the child to see if they know when they are beginning to get upset by something. Help them to identify the physical aspects of their feelings, i.e. a rush of energy, a feeling they might cry, not knowing what to do next, not being able to 'think straight', heart beating fast, breathing fast. Talk with them about what they might do instead of hitting out:
- go and get a drink
- go and visit an adult in the school
- put their hands in their pockets and count to ten etc.

☛ **Running away:** The paramount concern for the child is that she is kept safe. It may be useful for a child who often does this to be initially offered somewhere 'safe' to run to in the school. One way of doing this may be for her to take a written 'message' to someone. If a child does run out of the classroom she must not be able to get out of the school grounds. It is important that teachers find out why running away makes sense to the child – is she escaping from something or running towards something and what is the motivating factor? Ask the child to draw herself at home and at school and talk about the pictures, who is in them, who has been left out, has she drawn a good day or a bad day – what makes a day good or bad etc.

F) UNUSUAL AND/OR INAPPROPRIATE BEHAVIOURS

Innate difficulties: Sometimes it is very difficult indeed to identify problems which have a genetic component, especially if there are also environmental factors which appear to be contributing to difficulties. Children who have social communication and behavioural difficulties range from intelligent 'loners' whose communication is self absorbed rather than non existent to those who cannot cope with a social world at all and exhibit many other unusual behaviours. These children may be on the autistic continuum. Behaviours typical of autism are:

- strongly expressed fear of change, including minor deviations from routine
- disinterest/resistance in playing interactively with other children
- fixations on certain objects or activities
- ritualistic and repetitive behaviour
- self stimulating behaviour; e.g. hand-flapping
- lack of imaginative play
- an inability to understand that others have their own perceptions and feelings
- lack of imitative behaviour.

If these behaviours seem to describe the child then a Stage Three referral to the educational psychologist would be helpful. Concerns will need to be sensitively explored with parents including finding out whether there are similar difficulties at home. Parents will need to be reassured that their child's strangeness is not the result of anything that they have or have not done.

Immediate management strategies

Teachers will need to adapt their approach to such children. This is likely to entail a good deal of flexibility. Strategies such as positive attention and praise do not work in the same way as they do with other children.

- ☛ Regular routines are helpful.
- ☛ Clear warnings of a change of activity or a change of routine will help to limit distress.
- ☛ Where possible, planning changes so that only one occurs at a time and new routines are firmly established before further changes are introduced.
- ☛ Pupils should be encouraged to work alongside but not necessarily with other children.
- ☛ Children's own interests could form a base for developing further skills.

Selective mutism
Some children choose not to talk at school. The first thing to do is to find

out whether the child is choosing to talk elsewhere and whether there are concerns about their hearing and/or language development. If this is not a problem then it is likely to be a question of confidence. Children at the early stages of learning another language are sometimes unwilling to speak in some situations until they have become more confident in their skills and familiar with new surroundings.

☛ Encourage the child to communicate by other non-verbal means, including playing non-verbal games.
☛ Introduce some puppet play within a small, regular group.
☛ It may be worth having a family member with whom the child will speak to spend some time in the class to break down the barriers between school and home. This is more likely to be successful with a sibling rather than a parent. Pressure to talk is likely to be counter productive.

Child sexual abuse

If a child's play, language or interactions with other children indicate an unusually high level of sexual knowledge then schools need to be vigilant and systematic in gathering information which can be collated to give good grounds for an investigation. It is vital not to jump to conclusions but keep an open mind without dismissing the possibility of abuse. The perpetrators of abuse could be anyone that the child has contact with, including siblings, and it may be that they have seen inappropriate activity or pornographic material, rather than experienced direct abuse themselves. This raises another set of concerns. If the child has been abused then their own emotional state is likely to be very volatile. In all schools there should be a clear policy and a named member of staff with responsibility for such matters. Local education authorities have procedural guidelines which advise actions to take. Unless there is a disclosure or physical damage to a child social services require substantial evidence of concern before they are able to act.

Child Protection: There are some excellent materials on the market which raise children's awareness of their rights to protection. See the references and resources section at the back of the book.

The Code of Practice for Special Educational Needs

Moving quickly through the stages of assessment

This chapter deals with in-school assessment and ideas for interventions at Stage Two. These are intended to build on the strategies for positive management described in the earlier chapters. There are times, however when concerns persist despite the best efforts of the school. If there are indications of innate disorders or child protection concerns that would require more specialist assessment and/or intervention it is possible to move quite quickly through the stages. Good information, however, will still be required before any decision can be made about further action and teachers are ideally placed to gather this in a systematic and sensitive way.

Full statutory assessment and statementing

Young children are at times statemented for behavioural difficulties but this step needs to be treated with caution for several reasons. Children change and develop rapidly at this age. If carefully planned and consistent interventions are in place teachers may well find that the behaviour they were worried about at the beginning of the statementing process is no longer their focus of concern at the end. Teachers strive to work closely with parents and for some families the initiation of formal procedures too soon may be counter productive. If the child has behavioural difficulties linked to innate factors it takes time for parents to come to terms with this. They may very well need to go through a grieving process, during which they may experience denial, anger, sadness and eventually acceptance. Teachers may be on the receiving end of some of this denial and anger, especially if they are seen as the bearers of difficult news. The statementing process also makes considerable demands on parents as well as teachers and they need to be in full, genuine agreement. Without parental cooperation it is difficult for the assessment to proceed smoothly. It is better for everyone to take the time to come to the decision together that statutory assessment is an appropriate and helpful way forward.

Some local authorities, however, continue to link all additional resources with statementing and it may be necessary to go through the process in order to get the help that is needed. This is most likely to be within-school support as special school provision for behavioural difficulties is less common for a child who is still very young.

Summary

Although some children come into school with behaviour which makes them particularly hard to manage in the infant classroom, their early experiences in school may make all the difference to how they are able to settle and learn.

This includes the attitudes of teachers towards them and how well they are accepted, the clarity with which their needs are identified, the approaches that are put in place to meet their needs and the consistency with strategies are employed to teach them more useful and appropriate behaviours.

INFANT CLASSROOM BEHAVIOUR: ASSESSMENT SCHEDULE

Section one: *Are any of the following contributing to the child's ability to cooperate?*

The child's ability to hear

Are there any indications that the child cannot always make out what is being said e.g. not responding, misunderstanding, looking blank?

When was the last hearing test?

The child's ability to see

Are there any indications that the child cannot see clearly? e.g. puts books close to his/her face, bumps into things, misjudges distance, screws his/her eyes up?

When was the last sight test?

Any known medical factors

Physical needs

Are there any indications that the child does not get enough sleep or is undernourished

The child's ability to understand the language used for classroom instruction

Are there records of earlier concern re language development?

Do parents/carers have concerns about language skills?

If the home language is not English how much exposure to English has the child had so far?

General learning difficulties

Are there indications that this child is behaving in all/most aspects of his/her development like a much younger child?

Events affecting the child's security e.g. a family breakdown, refugee experiences, bereavement, a new baby.

Relevant on-going factors e.g. child protection issues, child accommodated by the local authority, family health matters.

Would a multi-agency planning meeting be useful to enable those already involved to share information, discuss a support network and identify clear ways forward for that child in school? Others involved:

Any meetings must include the parent/carer and their participation must be facilitated by the following as required:

- Invitation to bring a friend
- Interpretation
- Child care support
- Awareness of literacy skills

Now go to Section Two to clarify areas in which it may be most helpful to intervene in the first instance.

Section two: *identifying areas of concern*

A (i) Learning needs

Does the child have problems with many skill areas?

Do they appear to forget easily, even when shown how to do something?

Are they more comfortable with activities which you would normally give to younger children?

What do parents say about how much time it takes their child to learn something new?

Learning Needs:

A Strength / No Concern / Some Concern / Major Concern.

A (ii) Language needs

Does the child have problems understanding what is said to him/her? Is he/she slow to follow instructions and relies on copying other children?

Does the child have difficulties expressing their needs, asking questions, conversing with peers? Does this lead to frustration for the child?

If their first language is not English can they understand and speak at an age appropriate level in their home language?

Language Skills:

A Strength / No Concern / Some Concern / Major Concern.

IF THE CHILD HAS LANGUAGE OR LEARNING NEEDS THEN THIS HAS TO BE TAKEN INTO ACCOUNT WITHIN ANY ACTION PLANS WHICH FOCUS ON THE FOLLOWING:

B. Social interactions

Is the child negative towards other children to the extent that this is interfering with his/her ability to collaborate with others?

Does the child appear to want friendships but not know how to relate positively to other children and this is causing distress to him/her and within the class generally?

Does the child make contact with peers in ways which alienate him/her from others.

Social Interactions:

A Strength / No Concern / Some Concern / Major Concern.

C. Settling to and completing work

Does the child's difficulty stem from inability to follow and comply with instructions?

Does the child's level of concentration and distraction mean that activities are seldom completed without a high level of adult support?

Is the child impulsive and 'fragmented', shifting from one activity to another and one thought to another?

Settling to Work:

A Strength / No Concern / Some Concern / Major Concern.

D. General disruptive behaviour

Does the child behave in ways that ensures that attention will be forthcoming either from adults or peers?

Does the child disturb others working / interrupt frequently during group activities?

Does the child behave in ways which are predominantly irritating rather than aggressive?

Disruption: No Concern / Some Concern / Major Concern.

E. Emotional distress

Does the child's behaviour appear to stem from perceptions of themselves and/or others that are exceptionally negative?

Does the child appear very unhappy, tense or anxious much of the time?

Does the child have sudden outbursts of aggressive/ distressed behaviour (for which there is not always an obvious cause?)

Emotional distress: Child usually cheerful and/or self-controlled / No concern / Some Concern / Major Concern.

F. Unusual/inappropriate behaviours

Does the child behave in ways that show a very low level of social awareness?

Are some behaviours ritualistic / obsessive or bizarre?

Is the child unwilling to communicate?

Are there other behaviours that are unusual?

Unusual behaviours: No Concerns/ Some Concern/ Major Concern.

CONCLUSIONS: In what areas does the child have most difficulty and what will be the initial focus of an individual education plan?

REFERENCES AND RESOURCES

References

Barahal, R., Waterman, J. and Martin, A.P. (1981) 'The social-cognitive development of abused children'. Journal of Consulting and Clinical Psychology. **49**, 508–516.

Barnes, P. (ed) (1995) *Personal, Social and Emotional Development of Children.* The Open University: Blackwell.

Blatchford, P. (1989) *Playtime in the Primary School.* Windsor: NFER–Nelson.

Blenkin, G. and Kelly A. (1996) *Early Childhood Education.* London:Chapman.

Bukowski, W., Newcomb, A. and Hartup W. (eds) (1996) *The Company they Keep: Friendship in Childhood and Adolescence.* Cambridge: Cambridge University Press.

Bullying: A Haringey Response. (1992) Haringey Education Authority.

Cicchetti, D., Ganiban, J. and Barnett, D. (1991) 'Contributions from the study of high risk populations to understanding the development of emotion regulation' In Garber, J. and Dodge, K.A. (eds) *The Development of Emotion Regulation and Dysregulation* (pp. 15–48) New York: Cambridge University.

Chazan , M. (1988) 'Bullying in the Infant School' in *Bullying in Schools.* Tattum, D. and Lane, D (eds). Staffordshire: Trentham Books.

Coll, L. (ed) (1990) *Vygotsky and Education: Instructional Implications and Applications of Sociohistorical Psychology.* Cambridge:Cambridge University Press.

Cowen, E.L., Pederson, A., Babigan, H., Izzo, L.D. and Trost M.A. (1973) 'Long-term follow-up of early detected vulnerable children', *Journal of Consulting and Clinical Psychology* **41**, 438–46.

Cowie, H. and Smith, P.K. (1992) Understanding Children's Development . Oxford: Blackwell.

Department for Education and Science (1989) *Discipline in Schools* (The Elton Report). London: HMSO.

Department for Education (1994) *Code of Practice for the Identification and Assessment of Special Educational Needs.* London: HMSO.

Dowling, M. and Downley, E. (1984) *Teaching 3–9 year olds. Theory into Practice.* UK: Ward Lock.

Dunn, J. (1987) 'Understanding feelings: the early stages' In Bruner, J. and Haste, H. (eds) *Making Sense: the child's construction of the world.* London: Methuen

Dunn, J. (1989) *Young Children's Close Relationships.* London: Sage.

Eisenberg, N., Fabes, R.A., Carlo, G. and Karbon, M. (1992) 'Emotional responsivity to others: Behavioural correlates and socialisation antecedents'. In *Emotion and its Regulation in Early Development.* San Francisco: Jossey Bass.

Eliot, M. (ed) (1991) *Bullying: A Practical Guide to Coping in Schools.* Harlow: Longman.

Fisher R. (1995) *Teaching Children to Learn.* Cheltenham: Stanley Thornes.

Flanagan, C. (1995) *Applying Psychology to Early Child Development.* London:

Hodder and Stoughton.

George, C. and Main, M. (1979) 'Social interactions of young abused children: Approach, avoidance and aggression' *Child Development*. **50**, 306–318.

Goleman, D. (1996) *Emotional Intelligence*. London: Bloomsbury.

Haringey Guidelines to Good Practice in the Early Years. Haringey Education Services.

Harter, S. and Buddin, B. (1987) 'Children's understanding of the simultaneity of two emotions: A five stage developmental sequence' *Developmental Psychology*, **23**, 388–399.

Imich, A. and Jeffries, K. (1987) 'Showing the Yellow Card'. *Times Educational Supplement*, 6th November.

Kamark, T.W., Manuck, S.B. and Jennings, J.R. (1990) 'Social support reduces cardiovascular reactivity to psychological challenge: a laboratory model' *Psychological Medicine*, **52**, 42–58.

Kohlberg, L. (1984) 'Essays on Moral Development', Vol. **2**, *The Psychology of Moral Development*. San Francisco: Harper and Row.

Lewis, M. and Saarni, C. (eds) (1985) *The Socialisation of Emotions*. New York: Plenum.

Lindahl, K.M. and Markman, H.J. (1993, March) 'Regulating negative affect in the family: Implications for dyadic and triadic family interactions'. Paper presented at biennial meeting of the Society for Research in Child Development, New Orleans.

Maslow, A. (1954) *Motivation and Personality*. New York: Harper and Row.

O'Reirdan, T. and Roffey, S. (1992) *Settling In and Getting Along in the Infant Classroom*. Published by Haringey Education Services.

Pluckrose, H. (1993) *Starting School – The Vital Years*. UK: Simon and Schuster.

Reynolds, D. (1985) Studying School Effectiveness. Lewes: The Falmer Press

Rickel, A. and LaRue, A. (1987) *Preventing Maladjustment from Infancy through Adolescence*. London:Sage.

Rogers, C. (1983) *Freedom to Learn*. Columbus: Charles E. Merrill.

Rubin, Z. (1980) *Children's Friendships*. Somerset: Open Books.

Saarni, C. (1979) 'Children's understanding of the display rules for expressive behaviour' *Developmental Psychology*, **15**, 424–429.

Salmon, P. (1995) *Psychology in the Classroom: Reconstructing Teachers and Learners*. London: Cassell.

SCAA. (1996) *Desirable Outcomes for Children's Learning*. London: DFE,

Scherer , K.R. (1979) 'Non linguistic indicators of emotion and psychopathology' In Izard, C.E. (ed) *Emotions in Personality and Psychopathology*, 495–529, New York: Plenum.

Tizard, B., Blatchford, P., Borke, J., Farquhar, C. and Plewes, I. (1988) *Young Children at School in the Inner City*. New Jersey: Lawrence Erhbaum Associates.

Turner, P. and Hammer, J. (1994) *Child Development and Early Education*. Mass.: Allyn and Bacon.

Varma, V. (ed) (1993) *Coping with Unhappy Children*. London: Cassell.

Wood, D. (1988) *How Children Think and Learn*. Oxford: Basil Blackwell Ltd.

Resources

These books contain ideas for practical strategies in the classroom and/or playground

Ayers, A., Clark, D., and Murray, A. (1995) *Perspectives On Behaviour*. London: Fulton.

Bliss, T. and Tetley, J. (1993) *Circle Time for Infant, Junior and Secondary Schools*. Bristol: Lame Duck Publishing.

Canfield, J. and Wells, H.C. (1994) *100 Ways To Enhance Self-Esteem In The Classroom*. Mass.: Allyn and Bacon .

Canter, L. (1992) *Assertive Discipline*. USA: Lee Canter & Associates.

Curry, M. and Bromfield, C. (1994) *Personal and Social Education In Primary Schools through Circle Time*. Stafford UK: NASEN

David, T. (1993) *Child Protection and Early Years Teachers*. Milton Keynes: Open University.

Dowling, M. (1995) *Starting School at 4: A Shared Endeavour*. London:Chapman.

Frederickson, N. (1991) 'Children can be so cruel – helping the rejected child' In Lindsay, G. and Miller, A. *Psychological Services for Primary Schools*. Harlow: Longman.

KIDSCAPE: Programmes for schools on dealing with bullying and keeping safe. Available from World Trade Centre, Europe House, London E1 9AA

Maines, B. and Robinson, G. (1992) *Michael's Been Bullied – Here's What to do....The No-Blame Approach*. Bristol: Lame Duck Publishing (training materials and video)

Maines, B. and Robinson, G. (1991) *Punishment: The milder the better*. Bristol: Lame Duck Publishing.

Maines, B. and Robinson, G. (1991) *Teacher Talk*. Bristol: Lame Duck Publishing.

Maines, B. and Robinson, G. (1991) *You Know You Can*. Bristol: Lame Duck Publishing.

Masheder, M. (1989) *Let's Cooperate*. London:Peace Education Project.

Mathias, B. and Spiers, D. (1992) *A Handbook on Death and Bereavement: Helping Children Understand*. National Library for The Handicapped Child.

Mosley, J. (1993) *Turn Your School Around*. Cambridge: L.D.A.

Mosley, J. (1996) *Quality Circle Time*. Cambridge: L.D.A.

Roffey, S., Tarrant, A. and Majors, K. (1994) *Young Friends: Schools And Friendship*. London: Cassell.

Rogers, B. (1994) *Behaviour Recovery: A Whole School Program For Mainstream Schools*. Harlow: Longman.

Ross, C. and Ryan, A. (1990) *Can I Stay in Today, Miss?* Staffordshire: Trentham Books.

Rutter, J. (1994) *Refugee Children in the Classroom*. Staffordshire: Trentham Books.

Saifer, S. (1990) *Practical Solutions To Practically Every Problem: The Early Childhood Teachers Manual*. NZ: Pademelon Press.

Shapiro, L. (1993) *The Building Blocks Of Self-Esteem: Activity Book*. King of Prussia, USA: The Center for Applied Psychology.

Wallace, F. and Caesar, D. (1995) *Not You Again....! Helping Children Improve Playtime And Lunchtime Behaviour*. Bristol: Lame Duck Publishing.

Westmacott, E.V.S. and Cameron, R.J. (1981) *Behaviour Can Change*. Basingstoke: Macmillan Education.

Wichert, S. (1988) *Keeping The Peace: Practising Co-Operation And Conflict Resolution With Pre-Schoolers*. Philadelphia: New Society.

White, M. (1995) *Raising Self Esteem – 50 Activities*. Cambridge: Daniels.

Wolfendale, S. (ed) (1989) Parental Involvement , Developing Networks between School, Home and Community. London: Cassell .

Zimmerman, T. (1995) *The Cooperation Workbook*. King of Prussia, USA: The Center for Applied Psychology.

Stamps and stickers etc.

Certificates for photocopying from *Celebrations*. Bristol: Lucky Duck Publishing.

Incentive stampers from *GLS Fairway*, Educational Suppliers.

Merit stickers and self-inking merit stampers from *Galt Educational*.

Stampers, stickers and certificates from *Super Stickers, Co.* Tyrone, Ireland Tel/Fax (016625) 57438.

Stickers from *Teaching Trends*, East Finchley. 0181–444 4473.

Books for Children

Aliki (1987) *Feelings* Pan Books

Brown, L. and Brown, M. (1988) *Dinosaurs Divorce: A Guide for Changing Families*. London: Little, Brown and Company

Heegaard, M.(1988) *When Someone Very Special Dies: Children Can Learn to Cope with Grief*. Minneapolis: Woodland Press

Heegaard, M. (1991) *When Mum and Dad Separate: Children Can Learn to Cope with Grief from Divorce*. Minneapolis: Woodland Press.

Mellonie, B. and Ingpen, R. (1987) *Beginnings and Endings with Lifetimes In Between*. Dragon's World

Mills, J. (1993) *Gentle Willow. A story for children about dying*. New York: Magination Press

Osman, T. and Carey. J. (1990) *Where has Daddy Gone?* London: Mammoth Books

Petty, K. and Firmin, C. (1992) Playground Series. London: Bracken Books. *Making Friends. Playing the Game. Being Bullied. Being Left Out.*